Pra

Captain Mor

"To use Paul's analogy of milk before meat, the text of this book goes down like rich chocolate milk. Spencer discusses the topic like a knowledgeable battlefield tour guide. He provides a good explanation of the war chapters and associated nuggets. The pictures and maps, combined with a comprehensive but conversational tone, will engage new readers and those who might feel daunted by the subject. I imagine this book acting as a hook for more serious study, a book that should be read by policy makers and generals."

—Morgan Deane, author of *Bleached Bones and
Wicked Serpents: Ancient Warfare in the Book of Mormon*

"I was a British soldier. After a few weeks as a conscript in artillery, I was commissioned into signals and served the remainder of my two years in that branch, partly in Cyprus (during the EOKA emergency), working for the air force, and partly in Jordan. After quitting full-time service, I volunteered for the part-time Territorial Army and served another twenty-six years.

"So, with my breadth of experience and with a lifelong interest in the technicalities of soldiering, I feel able to look at *Captain Moroni's Command* with more than just a casual approach. It's brilliant! David Spencer captures the scenarios, the personalities, and the technicalities to a nicety. Even to a nonmember, this work is filled with interest."

—Major Hugh M. Jones, author of www.battlefieldreview.com

CAPTAIN
MORONI'S
COMMAND

DAVID E. SPENCER

CAPTAIN
MORONI'S
COMMAND

DYNAMICS OF WARFARE
IN THE BOOK OF MORMON

CFI
An Imprint of Cedar Fort, Inc.
Springville, Utah

ISBN 13: 978-1-4621-1540-2

Published by CFI, an imprint of Cedar Fort, Inc.
2373 W. 700 S., Springville, UT 84663
Distributed by Cedar Fort, Inc., www.cedarfort.com

LIBRARY OF CONGRESS CATALOGING-IN-PUBLICATION DATA

SPENCER, DAVID ELLIOTT, 1964- AUTHOR.
Captain Moroni's command / David Elliott Spencer.
   pages cm
ISBN 978-1-4621-1540-2
1. Moroni, Captain (Book of Mormon figure) 2. Book of Mormon--Criticism, interpretation, etc. 3. War--Religious aspects--Mormon Church. 4. War--Religious aspects--Church of Jesus Christ of Latter-day Saints. 5. Mormon Church--Doctrines. 6. Church of Jesus Christ of Latter-day Saints--Doctrines. I. Title.

BX8627.4.M75S64 2015
289.3'22--dc23

2014049835

Cover design by Shawnda T. Craig
Cover design © 2015 Lyle Mortimer
Edited and typeset by Kevin Haws

Printed in the United States of America

10 9 8 7 6 5 4 3 2 1

Printed on acid-free paper

Dedication

This book is dedicated to Dr. Philip Flammer, professor of military history at Brigham Young University, whose course on the dynamics of war, personal interest in me, and kindness opened my eyes and set the course of my professional career. This book would not have been possible without you.

Contents

Acknowledgments

S pecial thanks to Jim Zackrison, a Seventh-day Adventist and fellow Latin American military historian who read the war chapters in Alma and this manuscript, therefore contributing an informed, open-minded point of view. To my brother Steven Spencer for his edits. To David Hamblin, who read the first—and incredibly bad—drafts and was still encouraging. To my brother Robert Spencer, who did the first layout for the book. To my wife, Linda, and children, Robert and Rebecca, who tolerated hours and hours of neglect to let me work on the text. And finally to everyone else who contributed in some fashion to the writing and production of this work.

Introduction

When I was a kid, I didn't enjoy reading the scriptures. It wasn't that I was uninterested in spiritual things; it was the reading part that was difficult for me. I was a kid who liked to be outdoors, so reading was pretty low on my priorities list. The arcane words and old-style poetic language of the scriptures did nothing to increase my interest. For a young boy, they were almost incomprehensible—absolutely nothing like the language that I was used to in the books in school about Dick, Jane, Spot, and the Cat in the Hat. What little I did like to read was about action, and I didn't perceive a lot of action in the scriptures—that is until I discovered the Book of Mormon. This book had plenty of action in it, particularly warfare.

This was especially appealing to me because, from as early as I can remember, I have been fascinated by all things military. I don't know why, I just was and continue to be to this day. The only Christmas that I remember clearly before I was seven was my fourth Christmas in Venezuela (my family lived overseas much of my childhood)—the morning I found my first G.I. Joe in my stocking. My brother and I both got them. I played and played with that doll (or action figure, as people prefer to call them today) and several subsequent G.I. Joes, which were my favorite toys until I was eleven. Another experience that year in Venezuela that is stuck in my memory was driving by a military base and seeing a ramrod-straight sentry in an olive green uniform, stiff ranger cap, and tall, shiny black combat boots. I had seen soldiers before and there was nothing remarkable about this one, but for some reason the image of that young man—particularly his boots—made a big impression on me. These early experiences set the course for my life.

Naturally, with my interest in all things military, the accounts of warfare in the Book of Mormon attracted me. It was reading about the battles that got me through the book the first time, because no matter how dull the book got (to an eleven-year-old boy), I could usually count on another good war story a few pages later. As I got older, I grew to better understand and appreciate the spiritual content of the book, but I always retained a fondness for those war accounts from that first reading. However, though there were many good battle stories in the Book of Mormon, a larger understanding of the political and military context eluded me. The accounts were not easy to understand, probably because the main purpose of the Book of Mormon is not to tell military history; it is to discuss God's dealings with several ancient peoples on the American continent. Details of the more mundane aspects of Nephite-Lamanite society are described usually only to help readers understand the context of the main spiritual story.

Sometimes fairly significant information from a historical point of view is mentioned only briefly as afterthoughts or casually in passing. And furthermore, because the Book of Mormon is an abridgement or summary of other accounts, there are immense gaps in the records due to spatial constraints. Finally, though there are many geographic descriptors, there is no map, and the named locations in the book aren't like any on any known map available to me. Even though the events in the book all happened on the American continent, where exactly on the continent continues to be a mystery (though there are some pretty good candidate locations). The lack of a map and the abridgment gaps make Book of Mormon war accounts fairly difficult to understand at anything more than a tactical level. For the most part, at the strategic and political levels—the larger context behind the accounts—they are deficient. So while I always enjoyed reading the war accounts, there was a level of understanding that was missing. This was frustrating to me as a reader who is trained in the study of political-military affairs.

In my life, I continued to study political and military science. I did my field work on the ground in Central America in the 1980s and Colombia in the 1990s. As I progressed in my learning, I sat down one day and decided to really try and apply my knowledge of these subjects to the war accounts in the Book of Mormon. I wanted to understand the big picture for myself, based on the premise that I had enough knowledge and education to figure it out. This journey began over a decade ago. A great deal of the raw work was done in the first year when I was a poor graduate student with more time on my hands, but as I learned more and more over the years, I refined my understanding and analysis.

I don't pretend to be an archaeologist, antiquarian, or to even be knowledgeable about ancient cultures and languages. Thus, this isn't a work about how Book of Mormon military practices compare to ancient Hebrew, Egyptian, Mayan, or Aztec military customs and practices. I'm a political scientist by training and a defense analyst by profession. I was also briefly an enlisted man in the military. This gave me a small dose of empirical experience. This book attempts to analyze the political and military dynamics in the war accounts based on the assumption that though armed conflicts differ from country to country, from culture to culture, and from one age to the next, there are certain fundamental principles, patterns, and dynamics that remain constant across all of these divides. The interaction and dynamics of terrain, leadership, technology, escalation, politics, logistics, strategy, operations, and tactics have a significant impact on the course and outcome of every war. And once the unique characteristics of each situation are accounted for, the above-mentioned dynamics tend to develop in consistent and logical patterns.

The major assumption behind this work is that because of these similarities, if one understands the fundamentals, a relatively accurate analysis of any war from any time can be done. It's in this context of identifying, understanding, and explaining these elements that this study was conducted. And most important, if the accounts of warfare in the Book of Mormon are authentic and not merely a product of the Prophet Joseph Smith's imagination, not only would these elements be present, but they would also interact and develop in ways that are consistent with similar dynamics of war present in political-military history throughout time. At minimum, this book should help members better understand a significant portion of the Book of Mormon that is often ignored or skimmed through. At most, it could serve to help convince skeptics and unbelievers to give the Book of Mormon a more serious look.

One important area that this book can contribute to, because of these dynamics, is the debate about Book of Mormon authorship. It would be hard for someone writing fiction—even someone with a profound understanding of the dynamics of war—to be able to write a convincing military account without forcing the reader to suspend belief at some point to maintain interest in the story. During part of my career, I designed realistic military exercises. I can say pretty categorically that writing a totally fictional military account that is one hundred percent convincing is almost impossible. As realistic as the scenarios are written, there is always an element of what we called "fairy dust." Eliminating or reducing the fairy dust to zero is the Holy Grail of exercise-scenario writers. The closer to the Holy Grail, the better the exercise. Even the written works of master military fiction writers like Tom Clancy require readers to exercise some degree of suspended disbelief. They get away with it because everybody knows their works are fiction, and therefore a degree of fairy dust is acceptable to make the stories flow.

Now imagine the difficulty of writing a work filled with complex political and military dynamics and having the gall to claim it was fact. Eliminating *most* fairy dust is superbly difficult for the master military novelists. Now imagine the difficulty of having this not as the main story of the work, but as the backdrop—a secondary story, though a pretty busy one—and still getting all the details right. This would be a supremely difficult task for experienced fiction writers, and an even more difficult process for someone without significant education or military knowledge like Joseph Smith, Oliver Cowdery, Sidney Rigdon, Ethan Smith, or Solomon Spaulding, all of the whom have been proposed as the real authors or contributing authors to the Book of Mormon. The presence, accuracy, and consistency of these dynamics would not necessarily prove the divinity of the Book of Mormon, but they would make Joseph Smith's claim that he translated the book from the original source with otherworldly assistance more plausible. And they would further open up the possibility that the book is indeed what Joseph Smith claimed it was: an ancient record of an ancient people. However, even if this was proved beyond any reasonable doubt, whether the account and the translation are of divine origin or not is still a matter of personal discovery and faith. The presence of sophisticated war dynamics merely add another layer to the foundation that makes the leap of faith not only possible but also easier.

This study in no way pretends to be the definitive word on this subject. However, I am fairly certain this is one of the first published works on warfare in the Book of Mormon from this particular approach. The aspiration of this work is to make a contribution to the greater understanding of warfare in the Book of Mormon, a contribution that can serve as a building block for far more brilliant and insightful minds than my own. At a minimum, I hope it keeps discussion on and interest in this subject alive. Warfare is probably one of the lesser-studied parts of the text, which is a something of a loss because such a large portion of the book discusses it.

While my original effort started over a decade ago and covered all Book of Mormon wars, the asymmetry of detail available for most of the book's military history compared to the period that Captain Moroni was the commander of all Nephite forces led me to focus this work specifically on the wars described in the war chapters in the book of Alma. The richness of the accounts is particularly friendly to the analysis I performed because the detail in the text leaves less open to speculation. Perhaps a more global analysis of Book of Mormon warfare will follow at a later date, but for now I will deal exclusively with Captain Moroni.

Timeline

Year (of the reign of the judges)	Western Theater	Main Event	Eastern Theater
18th	Battle of Sidon River Crossing	The invasion of the Zoramites and Lamanites	
19th	Battle of Noah	Amalickiah becomes king of the Lamanites (first Lamanite campaign)	
20th			
21st			
22nd			
23rd			
24th			
25th	King Men rebellion and Amalickiah's armies take the cities of Manti, Cumeni, Zeezrom, Antiparah	Second Lamanite campaign	Amalickiah's armies take several cities and Teancum slays him (on last day of the year)
26th			
27th	Antiparah Maneuver		
28th	The siege and fall of Antiparah		Battle of Mulek
29th	Battles of Cumeni and Manti	Third Lamanite campaign	Battle of Gid and the Lamanites take over Nephihah
30th			
31st			Battles of Nephihah and Moroni

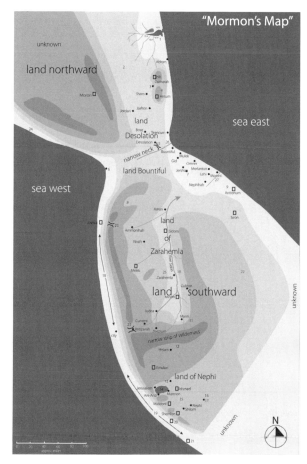

Legend

- Settlement
- □ Land with no city mentioned
-)(Mountain pass
- ⟿ Swamp

River tributaries are illustrative only. The darker colors indicate higher elevation.

John L. Sorenson. *Mormon's Map* (Provo: Farms, 2000).

Legend (continued)

1. Waters of Ripliancum
2. Limit of Nephite retreat
3. Shiz's death; plates left
4. Hill Shim
5. Narrow pass or passage
6. Hagoth's ship-building site
7. Camp of Moroni
8. Nephite refuge (3 Nephi 3:23, 25)
9. Hill Omni
10. Hill Amnihu
11. Hill Riplah
12. Valley of Alma
13. Dispersal of the sons of Mosiah
14. Waters of Mormon
15. Hill north of Shilom
16. Mount Antipas
17. Place Onidah
18. Wilderness west of Zarahemla
19. Wilderness west of Nephi
20. Lamanite king's land
21. Land of first inheritance
22. Wilderness
23. Mountain pass
24. Hagoth's likely destination
25. Wilderness of Hermounts
26. Divide of Desolation and Bountiful
27. Defense line

Setting the Stage

Chapter 1: Captain Moroni's Genius

Two military campaigns are described in greater detail than any others in the Book of Mormon, largely revolving around the man who led the Nephite armies: Captain Moroni. It is evident that Mormon, the compiler of the text, was something of an admirer of Captain Moroni, as he offered this praise: "Yea, verily, verily I say unto you, if all men had been, and were, and ever would be, like unto Moroni, behold, the very powers of hell would have been shaken forever; yea, the devil would never have power over the hearts of the children of men" (Alma 48:17).

No other major figure in the rest of the book is granted that high of an accolade. Especially intriguing in a religious book, this could be seen as an unusual compliment for a military man, one who spent most of his adult life continuously at war. Captain Moroni made no prophecies and performed no miracles, both accomplished by a number of others throughout the work.

Despite this, it's easy enough to understand why Mormon admired Captain Moroni more than just about any other person mentioned in the work. Part of the explanation is no doubt due to who Mormon was. He had been made a military commander at the age of sixteen (Mormon 2:2), and to the time of his death he was almost constantly at war—most of the time leading his doomed people into battle. With that kind of life and background, it's understandable how the accounts of Captain Moroni were Mormon's particular favorites and a source of great inspiration and comfort to him because they showed how an individual, particularly a military officer, could remain true to and favored of God despite being thrust into the ugliness of war. It is almost certain that Mormon saw a lot of parallels between his own life and the life of Captain Moroni. Mormon's admiration extended into his personal life, as he likely named his son after his great hero. Mormon's son Moroni also became a military officer and a captain of thousands (Mormon 6:12).

As the Book of Mormon was written for the latter days (Mormon 3:17–22), Captain Moroni is an example worth emulating, especially for members who are currently serving in the military. The fundamental theme of Captain Moroni's service is that it's possible for individuals heavily involved in war to still retain their ideals and avoid descent to the depredations often associated with armed conflict.

What were Captain Moroni's attributes that made him so great? In Alma 48:11–13, Mormon gives us some clues: he was physically strong and mighty, intelligent, and a patriot in the sense that he was willing to fight and dedicate his life to the freedom and liberty of his country; however (and this is key), he did not delight in bloodshed (verse 11). He was a religious man, one who feared God and recognized His hand in all things, especially his victories. In other words, he acknowledged his total dependence on God to win. He felt so strongly about his faith that he was willing to give his life so that others might enjoy the right to worship (verses 12, 13). Finally, and above all, he was a hard worker and was constantly involved in improving the defenses of his people (verse 12). He faced problems head on wherever he found them and never held back.

What else is known about him? From the remainder of the account, we know that he was a man of action. He led many armies personally and was wounded in battle (Alma 52:35). He cared deeply for his men and was enraged when he thought they were being mistreated by the government. A typical soldier, he hated bureaucracy, especially when it affected his soldiers' lives. He had a temper and could be impulsive, often when confronted by real or perceived incompetence and wickedness that caused innocents to die or suffer in misery (Alma 59:13). He could be judgmental and critical if he thought a person deserved it, as can be seen by the letters that he wrote to Ammoron, the enemy leader, and Pahoran, Moroni's own political leader (Alma 54:5–14; 60).

Modern-day officers have lost their careers for milder words directed in anger at their political leaders, particularly if they prove to be wrong. This willingness to confront what he saw as evil and incompetence indicates a far greater concern for the task at hand than his personal advancement.

In contrast to how he treated those he held in contempt, Captain Moroni displayed strong fraternal feelings for those he esteemed, being incredibly close to his comrades in arms. This showed clearly with his subordinate commanders Teancum and Lehi (Alma 53:2). In today's world, Moroni would be considered a soldier's soldier, meaning a man who leads from the front, shares the deprivations of his men, puts his mission and men above himself, and never asks his subordinates to do things he is not willing to do himself. Modern military commanders could learn a thing or two about integrity by studying him.

Captain Moroni was also a military genius, possessing a knack for developing new technology and tactics to give his forces a competitive edge on the battlefield, thus managing to stay one step ahead of his foes. And he was particularly adept at developing ingenious—not to mention innovative—application methods of time-tried principles of war. The most outstanding examples of his genius were the development of field works and body armor for his troops.

Both armor and fortifications were well known. The Nephites knew of armor from Palestine. Nephi, for example, had worn Laban's armor (1 Nephi 4:19), and cities had been surrounded by walls and protections in Lehi's day (1 Nephi 4:4), so these would most likely have been familiar to Nephite military leaders. If we assume that Central America was the Nephite's home, the terrain, resources available, and climate were quite different from Palestine. The types of body armor and fortifications employed in the Middle East were not necessarily practical, available, or efficient in the New World setting, as Spanish forces found out during their wars of conquest in the sixteenth century. Captain Moroni's genius lay not in inventing fortifications and armor, but rather in developing armor and fortifications that were cheap, practical, and could be used efficiently in his environment. In other words, they were effective and could be mass produced, where previously their production of such things may have been a slow and costly process.

Armor

Breastplates and other armor were a part of battle from the times of Nephi. However, prior to Moroni's time, they did not seem to be used generally and didn't figure prominently in any of the previous war accounts. Perhaps this was because at that time in the Nephite civilization, each individual was responsible for equipping himself for war. Metal armor was probably incredibly expensive, slow to make, cumbersome, and unsuited to the tropical climate, thus making it impractical for use in battle except for in special circumstances. From various accounts in the text, it can be said a large professional army was not maintained. Only a small cadre of professional officers and fighting men remained permanently on duty. This professional force was designed to be the first line of defense and form the backbone of a rapidly mobilized citizen's army in the event of major war.

Armies were mobilized when circumstances required. When wars broke out, preparations were frantically made, primarily by producing weapons and distributing them to citizen soldiers or militias (Mosiah 9:15–16; Alma 2:12–13). Because of this type of organization, time was precious, perhaps too short to produce much armor. This indicates that the use of armor prior to Captain Moroni's time was probably rare and only worn by leaders, professional officers, and wealthy men.[1]

Captain Moroni made an important innovation when he insisted that his entire army wear armor. The accounts say this wasn't necessarily metal armor, but consisted of thick clothing reinforced by rigid plates at critical junctions. The text talks of breastplates, arm-shields, and head shields (Alma 43:18). If Central America is indeed the land of the Book of Mormon, the thick clothing was likely similar to that worn by Aztec and Mayan warriors. This armor consisted of a quilted cotton waistcoat that the Spaniards reported was much cooler and more comfortable than their own metal breastplates were and that it resisted the penetration of arrows and stones nearly as well.[2]

---

1. The priority imposed by this method of preparing for war is known today as "just in time" logistics and would have emphasized the production of weapons, ammunition, and supplies.

2. Beatriz Repetto Tio, *Desarrollo Militar Entre los Mayas* (Yucatán, Mexico: Maldonado Editores, 1985), 38.

Statue of a Mayan soldier. He's armed with a two-edged sword and dressed just in a skirt. His protection consists of an elaborate feathered helmet and a small shield. The necklace may have provided some small protection for the upper chest. (The Guatemalan Military Museum, November 2006.)

Recreation of a northern Peruvian Moche warrior from the Book of Mormon time period. Armed with a copper club, he is only protected by a small round shield. (Callao Army Museum, July 2007.)

Recreation of a warrior from Colombia's pre-conquest period. Scantily clothed, his armor is largely symbolic, consisting of a thin gold breastplate and arm, leg, and headbands. (Colombian Military Museum, February 2008.)

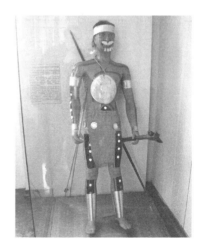

The plates of Captain Moroni's armor may have not been made of metal either, a fact consistent with archeological findings in the Americas, which indicates the use of metal was rare. Scarcity would prevent its general issue to thousands of troops. Moroni's uniform gave added protection, but the armor was by no means invulnerable against the weapons of the day. Armor is not generally designed to stop everything thrown at it; instead, it seeks to balance protection and offensive maneuverability, so Moroni's armor made penetration wounds and death more difficult, sacrificing absolute protection for economy and weight. Accounts indicate that if hit hard enough, the head plates could be split in two and the breastplates pierced (Alma 43:44). Metal can be pierced, but it isn't usually broken in two by a blow unless it's made of low-quality material. The previously cited verse makes specific reference to the head plates, suggesting that they may have been made of something like wood—a material that, if hit hard enough, will break in two. The breastplates and arm plates may have been made of a single layer or multiple layers of rawhide, which could be pierced but not split in two. Rawhide, wood, and ceramics tend to be lighter than metal and are also cheaper to produce. The use of rawhide and wood for armor is consistent with the effort to keep the armor light and cheap to effectively deal with the problems of tropical weather and production costs.

Aztec shield displayed at the Chapultepec Castle museum.

Aztec armor of leather sewn onto quilted cotton at the Chapultepec Castle museum.

This photo shows a Mayan warrior drinking *chicha* before going into battle. His outfit is similar to those described in the Book of Mormon, with a helmet covering the head and ears, a quilted waistcoat, a thick collar covering neck and shoulders with a round chest plate to protect the heart and lungs, and a shield. Note also his banner identifying him as an individual and for which side he fights. (Museo Antropologico de El Salvador.)

Part of the body that was conspicuously unprotected by Moroni's armor was the legs. During the famous battle for the city of Noah, only fifty Nephites were wounded. All of the wounds were to the legs and, according to the account, "many were severe" (Alma 49:24). This same verse implies that the reason they suffered wounds on the legs was they were not covered and protected in the same way that their heads, chests, and arms were. This was probably done in the interest of keeping the armor light and minimizing loss of mobility.

The notion that Captain Moroni's design consisted of large metal protective plates covering the whole body is not consistent with the accounts. This type of suit would be nigh impossible to wear by even the strongest men for any length of time in a tropical environment. For that matter, heavy metal plate armor would be impractical just about anywhere in the Americas, particularly in the tropical lands of Central America or the mountainous terrain of the Andes, which are considered by many to be likely candidates for Book of Mormon lands. Marching up and down hills or mountains with heavy armor would push a man to exhaustion before he ever entered the battlefield.

Consistent with the archeological evidence, beasts of burden are never mentioned. This means that men had to carry everything on their backs, or they had servants who served as porters. So Moroni's

Aztec bronze and copper axe heads at the Chapultepec Castle museum.

armies were made up entirely of infantry men who had to march and countermarch long distances over rough terrain. Even in the flatter lands and temperate climates of Europe, infantry soldiers couldn't wear metal armor for long periods of time. Armor and heavy weapons were generally carried in baggage trains and donned only shortly before battle. Armies that, for a variety of circumstances, were forced to wear armor during the march invariably arrived to the battlefield exhausted and were consequently of little military value unless first given a rest. Not only is heavy metal armor for infantry expensive and impractical, but when soldiers are left to their own devices, they'll often discard whatever they think is useless encumbrance. Experience has repeatedly demonstrated that soldiers will only keep equipment they feel is indispensable to their immediate survival.

Captain Moroni's innovative armor was not only worn by the Nephites throughout the war, but subsequently the Lamanites adopted it as well. Enemies adopting equipment developed by their rivals is a good indication of usefulness. Moroni's genius is clear in the armor he developed—practical, cheap, and light enough for general issue to his fighting force. If geographical calculations are correct, his armor is probably the direct ancestor of Aztec and Mayan armor encountered by the Spaniards in the sixteenth century, showing historically the enduring practicality of Captain Moroni's developments.

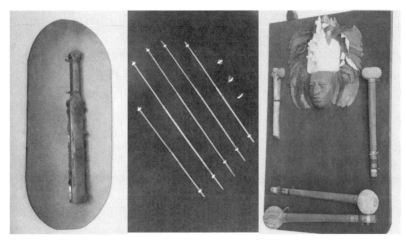

(Left to right) A Mayan sword, *atlatl* darts, and Mayan warrior weapons and feathered helmet used during the conquest period in Guatemala, consisting of stone-headed maces and an axe. (Municipal Museum of Antigua, August 2009.)

Photograph of a sign at the Etowah Indian Mounds in Georgia that depicts the theoretical construction of the defensive ditch at Etowah. (Etowah Indian Mounds Historic Site, Cartersville, Georgia, December 2007.)

Ingenious Fortifications

Captain Moroni's second major innovation was the development of ingenious fortifications, described in detail in Alma 50. Moroni had his men dig deep ditches around each city, piling up the dirt on the closest side in a continuous mound (Alma 49:2, 4, 18; 50:1). On the crest, he ordered a chest-high wall of wood built, presumably with logs (Alma 50:2). In front of this wall were what he called "pickets,"

The fortified bastion at Yorktown, Virginia, July 2008. The log spikes on the walls of the bastion are likely similar to the "pickets" of Captain Moroni's fortifications. This shouldn't pose a dilemma for the modern believer since principles of fortification are fairly constant across cultures and history.

which were probably sharpened and angled stakes stuck in the ground facing outward, designed to prevent the enemies from getting close enough to assault the wall (Alma 50:3). At strategic intervals, frame towers were erected and topped off with a protected turret that was perhaps covered in rawhide, wood, or some other arrow-resistant material. From there, archers and men with slings were stationed (Alma 50:4). These men were positioned high enough to completely overlook all the approaches to the ditch. Besides dominating the ditch with missile fire, the men in these towers would also serve as sentries who would warn the garrison where exactly the enemies were approaching to make their assault.

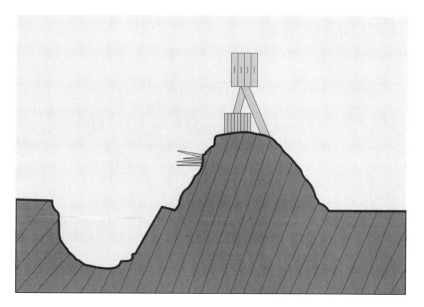

The above drawing by the author shows a profile view of Captain Moroni's innovative fortification. This included an outer ditch and mound surrounding the city with pickets embedded into the mound. At the crest of the mound, a high wall would be built with strategically placed frame towers overlooking the approaches to the ditch.

A common problem for most defenders of fortified positions is the inability to distribute their garrison to adequately defend all sectors of the fortifications. As a consequence, they have to take calculated risks and distribute their forces where they think the attack is most likely to happen while leaving other sectors either weakly garrisoned or even abandoned. The towers would've contributed to the defending commander's decision-making process by helping the commander see the enemies approaching and anticipate where their likely avenues of attack were. With that knowledge, he could quickly distribute his forces to reinforce threatened sectors before attackers could properly make their assault.

The only opening into the city was through a main entrance. The vulnerability of this gap was minimized by stationing the strongest and most heavily armored men to repel attackers (Alma 49:4, 18, 20). Moreover, the men in this narrow passage were probably supported by the stones and arrows shot by the men posted in the towers. While the accounts don't specifically say so, the ditch around the city was likely extended to the entrance as well, and there was probably some sort of bridge that could be placed or withdrawn as needed. Any attacker would first have to cross the ditch under the Nephite stones and arrows from the towers. After crossing the ditch, an attack would have to move through a narrow channel dominated by the towers and men posted behind the walls that was designed to limit the number of attackers that could advance abreast. This would create a shooting gallery within which there was little cover or escape.

Should attackers reach the entrance, they would then have to deal with the strong, heavily armored men. As long as the flanking defensive positions remained intact, only a few enemies at a time would've been able to reach the position of these strong men unscathed; most would not arrive, and those that did would be wounded and exhausted—easy prey for the defenders. The narrowness of the entrance also meant that the defenders could rapidly and easily rotate or reinforce their men at this entrance position while the attackers could do neither. In this way, Moroni employed the tried-and-true tactical principle that obstacles and fortifications are not always effectively employed when set up as absolute barriers. Their most effective use is dependent on designing them in such a way as to channel the enemy forces into terrain where the defenders' weapons can be brought to bear for maximum effect. In other words, a fort that channels attackers into the prepared kill zones. Captain Moroni designed all of the Nephite fortifications specifically for this purpose.

A view showing one of the two narrow entrances at Etowah. An example of a fortification designed to channel enemy forces into terrain where weapons can be used to their maximum effect. The entrance is at an angle, which makes it impossible for attackers to fire directly into the village. Also, it is dominated at the end by a bastion tower and flanked by palisade walls from which an attacker would've had to run through a gauntlet of projectile fire before even reaching the entrance. (Etowah Indian Mounds Historic Site, December 2007.)

The Lamanites under Amalickiah were rather astonished when they first encountered these fortifications, believing that they had leveled the playing field by adopting Captain Moroni's style of armor for all of their armies. They had assumed that by armoring up, they could use their numerical advantage to overwhelm the Nephites (Alma 49:6). However, Moroni did not underestimate his enemy (Alma 49:15). He understood how armies adapt and knew that his forces' armor would no longer be sufficient to give them the upper hand after Amalickiah and his men became familiar with his equipment. By developing field fortifications, Moroni stayed one step ahead of the Lamanites and again ingeniously compensated for the numerical disadvantage the Nephites faced. He ordered fortifications and walls to be thrown up around every Nephite city.

The Book of Mormon mentions city walls in earlier chapters. Most likely these walls were made of stone, requiring years of skilled labor to construct. Moroni's innovative fortifications showed his genius in using mounds of dirt topped with timber walls. These fortifications could be built quickly with unskilled labor. His adversary, Amalickiah, was a Nephite defector—as were most of his military leaders—but he was unacquainted with these fortifications, which indicates they had not been in place when Amalickiah and his men had gone over to the Lamanites. When Amalickiah came back with a large invading army a year or so later, all of the major cities had been fortified—a remarkable feat that wouldn't have been possible with stone walls.

The constant introduction of new tactical innovations and their adoption by both sides demonstrates the presence of an important dynamic of war: the process of escalation. The presence of this dynamic throughout the text supports the idea that the military accounts are authentic. It would've been difficult for Joseph Smith or any of his contemporaries, who had little military knowledge, to understand this and include it so consistently in the accounts of Book of Mormon warfare. Escalation of war is one of those subtle complexities found in the text that constantly argues against Joseph Smith's authorship.

A view showing one of the two narrow entrances at Etowah. The entrance is at an angle, making it impossible for attackers to fire directly into the village. Also, it is dominated at the end by a bastion tower and flanked by palisade walls from which attackers would have to run a gauntlet of projectile fire before reaching the inside of the fort, where they could easily be blocked by a group of select warriors. (Etowah Indian Mounds Historic Site.)

Aerial view of a narrow pass with a bridge that could be withdrawn if needed. (Etowah Indian Mounds Historic Site, December 2007.)

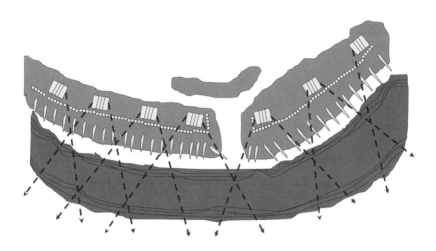

Above drawing by the author showing an aerial view of the towers all placed srategically to allow the city defenders to cover every approach to the ditch.

Model of the Etowah village fortification, which is remarkably similar to the system described in the Book of Mormon. In this case, an outer ring of nut tree orchards prevents flaming arrows from being shot in. A flooded man-made ditch meets with the Ohio River. The inner bank is topped with a twelve-foot palisade that's reinforced with square bastion towers at roughly eighty-foot intervals from which stones and arrows can be hurled at enemies. Etowah flourished from AD 1000–1550 and was part of the Mississippian culture. While Indian mounds were well known in Joseph Smith's time, knowledge of their culture and fortification systems were not. (Etowah Indian Mounds Historic Site, December 2007.)

An outer-earthen berm protecting the northwest side of the ruins of Iximche, Guatemala. Iximche is protected on its other sides by steep ravines. It was built in AD 1470 and was the capital of the Kaqchikel Mayans until the Spanish forced them to abandon it in 1526. (Iximche National Park, Guatemala, August 2009.)

The outer slope of the berm and what appears to be the remains of a ditch at Iximche. (Iximche National Park, Guatemala, August 2009.)

The remains of a defensive ditch at Ocmulgee, Georgia, another Mississippian fortified village in central Georgia. This one flourished from AD 900–1150. Trenches have been found to the north, northeast, south, and southeast of the site. (Ocmulgee National Monument, December 2007.)

The remains of the defensive ditch at Etowah. (Etowah Indian Mounds Historic Site, December 2007.)

Chapter 2: Military Systems

As mentioned previously, a small cadre of professional military officers and men were maintained by the Nephite government to lead their nation during times of war. This may have been a relatively new institution among the Nephites in Captain Moroni's time as only in the book of Alma does the war account first clearly identify the professional military officers among the Nephites. Moroni, Lehi, and Teancum appear to have been part of this institution, enjoying a relationship similar to a fraternity. Other officers are mentioned, such as Helaman, but they were definitely not part of the fraternity.

There may have been several reasons for this. Moroni, Lehi, and Teancum could've all been from the same geographical region, as all are connected to the northeastern coastal region. When Moroni raised the title of liberty, he prayed to God and declared all the land south of the land of Desolation a chosen land (Alma 46:11–18). This brings to mind an empowering image of Moroni standing at the edge of Desolation on the southern end of the narrow neck of land (or land of Bountiful), conducting this ceremony. A city on the eastern seashore, built at a later date to contain the Lamanites, was named after Captain Moroni. The Book of Mormon says it was the people's custom to name a land after the first person to inhabit it (Alma 8:7). This honor perhaps also applied to their prominent local citizens. If Moroni were from the area around Bountiful, it would make sense that a city would be named after him. By then, he was undeniably a prominent inhabitant. Throughout the war, Moroni seems to take a more personal interest in conducting and directing the war on the east coast than the west, an area he had entrusted into the hands of Helaman. Though the accounts lead the reader to conclude that the greatest Lamanite threat was on the eastern flank, Captain Moroni's interest may have also been personal.

Teancum is always mentioned in the Book of Mormon in connection with the northeastern coast. He protected the land of Bountiful—never leaving this theater—and fought all of his battles there. He died in the land of Bountiful, and the city that guarded the northern approaches was later named after him (Mormon 4:3).

Lehi isn't always mentioned in connection with the northeast, but a land may have been named after him there. The inhabitants of the land bearing this name later had a dispute with Morianton and his people (Alma 50:25–36). Lehi participated in two battles in the west: the Battle of Sidon Crossing and the Battle of the City of Noah. After the second battle, all subsequent mention of Lehi relates to the northeast. He is last mentioned defending the land of Bountiful from the army of Coriantumr, the Mulekite dissenter (Helaman 1:25–32). This common regional origin of professional military officers may be akin to the stronger tendency of southerners to become officers in the United States military than young men from other regions; or it could be that there was more conflict in this area, so more regional men became soldiers.

Helaman, on the other hand, was a different sort of leader—not a military leader by profession. During wartime, the majority of the soldiers and officers were recruited from the population on the basis of need and were maintained and equipped by the central government. From the story of Helaman's stripling warriors, we learn something of the formation and maintenance of citizen army units during times of war. Units were raised from a single geographical location and led by locally chosen officers. The men appointed their officers, generally choosing men with religious[3] and professional experience, meaning

---

3. It shouldn't be surprising that the religious leaders were chosen. Religion and politics were closely related, and though there were separate priests and judges in the Book of Mormon, the political implications of religion were enormous.

those with proven leadership attributes (Alma 56:3–9). In the same way that units were raised in a particular geographical location, that area was also responsible for providing replacement recruits and the supplies for their local units. The fathers of the stripling warriors sent them supplies and reinforcements (Alma 56:27).

However, the central government also played a role in providing additional supplies, equipment, and replacements. In the account of the stripling warriors, both men and supplies were continually being sent down from Zarahemla and elsewhere (Alma 56:28; 57:6; 58:4–8). One of Captain Moroni's vigorous protests to the central government occurs when he thinks the government isn't providing the necessary supplies and men to supplement local efforts (Alma 59).

Overall leadership of the armies was entrusted to the professional military men. It is fairly likely that the local units were stiffened by professional cadre or select units of regulars. It often seems that the militia units were reinforced and led by regular soldiers from the same geographical region. For example, when Lehi leads units from the northwest, Teancum is always mentioned in connection with units and battles in the northeast. A city is later built in this region with his name (Mormon 4:3). It's possible this is where they were both from.

While the initial leadership of the armies was given to regulars (peacetime soldiers), militia officers who proved particularly competent could rise to high levels of command. When Antipus (who may have been a regular) died, Helaman assumed the leadership of the whole southwestern littoral front (Alma 56:57). Helaman proved to be a brilliant commander, perhaps as skilled as Moroni, but he never received the same recognition. Perhaps this is because he was a priest turned sometime warrior. This kind of regular-versus-militia rivalry has plagued militaries since time immemorial, particularly when the militia units or leaders outshine the regulars. It's even possible that Mormon (a regular) favored Captain Moroni in the text over Helaman, despite the latter's apparent equal military brilliance. There is no Alma 48:11–13 equivalent for Helaman. Helaman's military talent is evident largely from the letter he wrote to Captain Moroni (Helaman 56–58) and not from Mormon's commentary.

It's not known exactly what system was used to choose captains, higher captains, and chief captains among the Nephites (Alma 2:13), nor what kind or what size units these officers controlled. It appears that, as said previously, the majority of the men were local militia-type units who elected their officers upon mobilization. However, some of the officers, particularly the top leaders, were professional officers who trained from their youth in the art of war and leadership. Soldiers who belonged to this caste often appear to have inherited their profession from their fathers. Among these professionals were Captain Moroni, Lehi, and Teancum. There were no doubt others as well—one example being probably Antipus—but only a few are mentioned by name in the text.

The following are sketches of the two most mentioned Nephite officers, after Moroni.

Lehi

Captain Lehi was born into a military family. He was the son of Zoram, who had once been the overall Nephite military commander, possibly Captain Moroni's immediate predecessor. Captain Lehi had at least one brother, Aha, who was also a military officer (Alma 16:5). Zoram and his two sons led a Nephite army on a successful surprise attack against a Lamanite army that had made its own surprise foray against the city of Ammonihah and land of Noah (Alma 16:5–7). The objective of the Nephite attack was to free the substantial number of captives lost to the Lamanites. In this they were entirely successful (Alma 16:2–8). You might wonder why, after this brilliant action, Lehi or Aha didn't subsequently take command of the Nephite armies, as it may have been common for sons to succeed their fathers in high office (see Helaman chapter 1). Aha isn't ever mentioned after this operation, though Lehi is the officer most often mentioned in the Book of Mormon after Captain Moroni. Moroni and Lehi were close friends throughout their military careers. The fact that they were close friends may speak volumes of Lehi's personality. He was likely eligible for the position of commander of all of the Nephite armies, but he remained in the army despite being passed over for the position in favor of Moroni. It could be that Aha was not as mature as Lehi and retired from military service. Maybe he did participate in the great war and is simply not mentioned again. Perhaps he died, and we are not told when or how.

Another possibility is Lehi was too old for command. Captain Moroni, his son Moronihah, and Mormon were all incredibly young when they took command of the Nephite armies. Captain Moroni was twenty-five (Alma 43:17). Moronihah was, at most, between twenty-four and twenty-seven years old[4] and possibly as even young as fourteen (Alma 62:43). Mormon was a teenager when he was appointed chief captain (Mormon 2:2). The reader gets the sense that Lehi was older than Moroni. This could be why Lehi was passed over in favor of Moroni. Regardless of the reason, Lehi was Moroni's most able subordinate commander throughout the Zoramite and the Amalickiahite wars. The two captains complemented each other well; while Moroni seems to have been the intellectual and the strategist, Lehi was the executor and master tactician and was present at most of the important battles.

Lehi's character is evident at the Battle of the Sidon Crossing. He was placed in charge of the delicate maneuver of keeping his forces hidden from enemy view in an exposed position across the river at the enemy's rear. He had to keep his nerve and remain hidden until the precise moment when called upon to trap the Lamanites in the river valley crossing between his and Moroni's forces. This job had to be entrusted to a mature and experienced commander because early detection would have meant the Lamanites destroying the exposed forces without getting caught in the trap. Moroni's force would have been stuck across the river, unable to help in a timely manner. If the trap were sprung too late, the Lamanites could have cut through Captain Moroni's forces (Alma 43:35) before Lehi could come to his aid. While the trap appears to have been sprung slightly early, Lehi's leadership allowed his force to keep the initiative and accomplish their task (Alma 43:40).

Evidently, Lehi was meticulously good at executing orders, as well as organizing plans. He kept his cool under pressure and was a steady and calm officer. He was probably the kind of man who, by his own personal serenity, inspired confidence in his troops. In almost every

---

4. He would have had to have been born when Moroni was fifteen and received command of the armies in either the 32nd or 35th year of the reign of the judges. Two years are mentioned in Alma 62.

subsequent battle where he is mentioned, Lehi's forces were assigned the most difficult maneuvers, the ones that required precision and nerve.

Lehi's reputation was greatly enhanced at the Battle of Noah, where Moroni made him commander of the city. New tactics always require a steady leader to test them, and Moroni chose Lehi, who lived up to his reputation and calmly employed the new style of fortifications to the greatest advantage against the assaulting Lamanites. As a result, he scored one of the most one-sided victories against the Lamanites recorded in the Book of Mormon (Alma 49:3–25).

Later on, Moroni sent Lehi to the eastern shore to help Teancum conduct the offensive operation against the Lamanites. In the Battle of Mulek, Moroni gave Teancum an assignment that required the most courage and aggression, but he gave Lehi the assignment that required the most skill and precision. Lehi carried out the assignment excellently. Again, it was Lehi's skill that carried the day (Alma 52).

Lehi and Teancum fought well together on the eastern shore, even bringing the war in that quarter to a successful conclusion. Teancum was killed when he took it upon himself to end the war and carried out the clandestine raid to assassinate Ammoron. Captain Moroni also died only a few years later. It's interesting that, of the trio, the probable eldest Captain Lehi lived the longest. This was most likely due to Lehi's serene and steady personality. Teancum had been on a course of self-destruction and Moroni was probably much more highly strung than Lehi, subject to much more stress as the military leader responsible for the fate of the whole nation. Thus, while Moroni aged tremendously under the burden of war leadership, Lehi seems to have felt the effects to a much lesser degree.

It's also interesting to note that Lehi continued to serve as an officer under the new commander Moronihah, the son of Moroni. In Moronihah's first war, the dissident Coriantumr made a surprise attack on Zarahemla and drove up the Sidon River valley to take Bountiful. Lehi was commanded to stop the Lamanites from taking it. Lehi met Coriantumr and, with his usual brilliance, stopped the Lamanite advance dead in its tracks (Helaman 1:28–29). This is the last mention of Captain Lehi in the Book of Mormon.

Teancum

If Lehi was the calm, steady commander, Teancum was his exact opposite. Teancum was fierce, aggressive, and impulsive. Moroni's appointed commander for the northeast littoral sector of the Nephite lands, Teancum is first mentioned pursuing and overtaking Morianton (Alma 50:25–36). He's next mentioned taking on the overwhelming armies of Amalickiah against immense odds (Alma 51:12, 28–32). Teancum apparently never shrunk from a fight and often displayed reckless courage in the face of the enemy, confronting the Lamanites with much smaller forces. However, his gambles almost always paid off with a victory. His greatest accomplishment was preventing the Lamanites from taking the vital city of Bountiful, which guarded the southern entrance to the narrow neck of land.

Teancum believed his men should be stronger and better trained than their enemies. He probably trained his men constantly to the point that they became a sort of special or shock force, a Nephite counterpart of the US Rangers. The scriptural account says that every one of Teancum's men "were great warriors" and "did exceed the Lamanites in their strength and in their skill of war" (Alma 51:31). Like Moroni, Teancum believed in leading by example. He probably shared all of the burdens his troops bore and would not ask them to do anything he wouldn't first do himself. The evidence for this is his willingness to take extreme personal risks to achieve strategic results. All of his qualities—his impulsiveness, courage, skill, and personal sacrifice—came together in two personal endeavors.

After the first day of the battle against Amalickiah's drive toward the city of Bountiful, Teancum took it upon himself to change the course of the war. He infiltrated the Lamanite camp at night, found Amalickiah's tent, and killed him with a javelin. Amalickiah died without a sound, and Teancum returned to his men. This personal act of courage—which under other circumstances might be called recklessness—probably saved the city, for when the Lamanites saw that their leader was slain, they lost heart and withdrew their assault (Alma 51:33–37). This single-handed act of bravery gave the Nephites the respite they needed to build up their strength for their own drive to recapture lost Nephite lands.

But the war did not end. Amalickiah's brother, Ammoron, who shared his goals, became the new Lamanite king. Slaying Amalickiah most likely made Teancum the most wanted Nephite commander by the Lamanites, which did not hinder Teancum from continuing to fight and take risks. When he got another chance, Teancum again took it upon himself to end the war. He again infiltrated the Lamanite camp, assassinating Ammoron. However, Ammoron cried out before he died, which alerted Ammoron's guards. They pursued Teancum and slew him (Alma 62:36). The death of Ammoron did produce the desired strategic impact, as it took the final spirit out of the Lamanite armies, ending the war. Teancum paid the ultimate price, but in the end his sacrifice saved countless other lives and consolidated strategic victory.

Because of his reckless personality, Moroni skillfully employed Teancum, assigning him the most precarious and dangerous missions. In the Battle of Mulek, he had Teancum to march by the city in plain sight with a small force shortly after he'd slain Amalickiah. Teancum coolly marched into the wolves' lair and back out again.

Teancum was skilled at rearguard actions, guerrilla hits and run attacks, and battles in open terrain; in other words, operations that required cunning, bravery, aggressiveness, and a willingness to fight alone against the odds. On the other hand, Teancum may not have been the most qualified for conducting attacks on fortified cities or operations that required organization, methodical planning, and patience. Teancum was ordered to attack and take the city of Mulek, but he instead waited for Moroni and Lehi to come to his aid, after which he participated as a subordinate commander when the city of Mulek was finally assaulted (Alma 52). Thereafter, Moroni never left Teancum alone in command. Instead, he ordered Lehi to aid Teancum in the offensive on the eastern shore. Perhaps Moroni didn't trust Teancum alone, but more likely he recognized that the combination of personalities would make a winning team. Whatever the case, the combination of Teancum and Lehi apparently worked well. Teancum provided the charismatic leadership, drive, daring, and aggressiveness needed to go on the offensive while Lehi provided the intellect (conceptual skill, planning, and administration) and the steadiness needed to conduct the campaign and properly manage the Nephite army.

The trio in many ways shared a remarkably similar relationship to some of the principal southern generals of the American Civil War. If Moroni were considered the Nephite version of General Lee (age notwithstanding), Lehi could be compared to the rock-steady Longstreet and Teancum to Lee's flamboyant and impetuous cavalry commander, J. E. B. Stuart. Like the South, the Nephites fought against an enemy superior in both in numbers and material goods. Lee's superior talent held the North at bay for four years; Moroni's superior ability held the Lamanites at bay for many years and eventually defeated them. Lee sent Longstreet to wherever the fighting was critical and required a mature and methodical leader; Moroni employed Lehi in the same way. Stuart was competent, but at the same time flamboyant and less reliable than Longstreet; Teancum seems to have been much the same. Finally, both Stuart and Teancum died in impetuous acts of daring while Lehi and Longstreet survived their individual wars and lived many years afterward. Something notable about this comparison is that the Book of Mormon appeared in print over thirty years before the commencement of the Civil War.

Chapter 3: Patterns of Conflict

The Book of Mormon wars generally followed consistent patterns. Normally, one side committed some act of war, after which both sides mobilized their armies—largely composed of citizen levees—and hastily manufactured weapons (for example, Alma 2:12–14). The Nephites usually defended their lands against Lamanite attacks, but not always. The attackers then chose one of a limited number of routes into the defending armies' land, preferring routes that allowed them to remain undetected for as long as possible, thus forcing the defenders to extend their forces by having to defend every route leading from the attackers' home bases.

For the attackers, this kept the defenders from concentrating their forces on one particular time and location, ceding the advantage to the attackers. The secrecy of this maneuver was likely aimed at concentrating enough forces in the opposite camp's territory for decisive battles before the other side could mobilize sufficient forces to block them, knowing that it would take days for the defending force to congregate. Sometimes the battles were meeting engagements and other times there was a formal agreement between the opposing leaders as to the time and location of the battle. Advantage was sought by outnumbering the opponent, choosing the terrain, or maneuvering tactically.

In order to counter the secret approach maneuver, the defending armies would attempt to intercept the attacking armies on ground that favored defense, relying on two methods: one pragmatic and the other prophetic. The pragmatic method involved what the Book of Mormon calls "spies"—in today's jargon, scouts (Mosiah 9:1; 10:7; Alma 2:21; 43:23–30; 58:14–20). The Lamanites also used spies to learn about Nephite troop concentrations. The prophetic method called for the commanders to approach prophets and priests, asking for inspiration and prophecy to divine their foes' route and intentions (Alma 43: 23).

Though it's never explicitly described in the text, battle conventions are implied often enough to take note of them. While not the norm during the war, Lamanite and Nephite armies often attempted to fight a single decisive battle rather than prolong the war or conduct a campaign with a series of engagements. This probably was derived from an old tradition and may have been seen as the more honorable form of war, with the battles being arranged—normally via written letters delivered by embassies or messengers (Alma 52:19). The letters challenged the opposite army to open battle at a specific time and place. Many times these invitations were refused, forcing a prolonged conflict (Alma 62:19; 52:20). When accepted, however, the battles were fought head to head during the day and, if there was no clear victory by one of the sides, the armies would withdraw at night and prepare to continue the next day.

Battles could be won by sheer force of numbers, by maneuvers and strategies, or some combination of them. Many Book of Mormon wars seem to have been won or lost in a single decisive engagement (see Mosiah 10; 20; Alma 2; 28; 43–44). The decisive battle may have been preceded by a period of harassment and raiding, which were all predominantly light engagements when compared to the climactic finale. Overall, this was the preferred method of conducting warfare, but it was a convention, not an unbreakable law. Though evidence suggests that attempts were made to follow the convention, both sides violated it when it favored them.

These battle conventions and dynamics are remarkably similar to conventions observed by the Greeks prior to the fourth century BC. Victor Hanson explains that these conventions were employed by the Greek agrarian societies in which land-owning farmers mobilized for war but then needed to return to their farms by harvest time.[5]

---

5. Victor Hanson, *A War like No Other* (New York: Random House, 2005), 24.

The convention of Greek Hoplite battle allowed wars to be decided in a major ritualistic engagement where the bloodiest battles resulted in less than 10 percent casualties of either force engaged. This convention tested societal manhood, created heroes, and decided political disputes, but it didn't interrupt the vital crop-growing cycle.[6]

Under this type of warfare convention, stealth, deception, and other forms of trickery were regarded as being underhanded and dishonorable. This is implied in the Book of Mormon by Mormon's constant apology and justification of Moroni's use of stratagem to fight the Lamanites. Mormon emphasizes that Moroni felt it was no sin to use stratagem in view of what was at stake for the Nephites (Alma 43:29–30). There is evidence that the Nephites attempted at times to observe convention, but when the Lamanites refused or the conditions were too unfavorable, Moroni resorted to stratagem (Alma 52; 58; 62).

Mormon apologized for Captain Moroni, noting that under the circumstances, the ends justified the means. Perhaps Mormon thought his readers would live in a day and age when the conventions of war were more honorable and would perhaps find Captain Moroni's actions reprehensible. Mormon's apology hardly registers today, because in the twenty-first century, soldiers' use of deception and stealth to win their battles is applauded. From today's view, there is absolutely nothing scandalous in what Moroni did. However, writing back in the fifth century, Mormon apparently felt a bit of guilt over Moroni's tactics. Perhaps Mormon's apology is more of a lament than a real apology, as Mormon himself lived in an era of total war and even greater unbridled savagery than the days of Captain Moroni. Mormon perhaps longed for a more civilized age.

In a similar vein, Hanson points out that the Peloponnesian War was extraordinary because it completely broke the Greek city state military conventions and forever changed the way war was fought. Thereafter, Greek poets and philosophers often lamented the bygone days of conventional Hoplite warfare, when fighting was glorious and honorable.[7] However, the reason the Peloponnesian War broke all the conventions was that more was at stake—the triumph of

---

6. Ibid., 133–34.

7. Ibid.

revolutionary imperial democracy versus the continuation of oligarchic government. From the military strategist's point of view, there was a great asymmetry between the two main contenders that led to such "unconventional" warfare. Sparta was a great land power and Athens was a great sea power, and each of them refused to meet the other on disadvantageous terms. Sparta refused until the end to engage Athens on the sea, and Athens refused to meet Sparta in a decisive engagement on land. Both sides thus sought to defeat the other—not by facing strength with strength in the way of convention—but by applying their respective strengths against their adversary's weakness, the essence of what Mormon calls *stratagem*. The result was the most brutal war in Greek history up to that time, lasting twenty-seven years, far beyond the single season of conventionally honorable wars of the past.

Similarly, the threat posed to Nephite society by Amalickiah was a high-stakes affair. It wasn't just a punishment raid, the possession of a piece of land, or the payment of tribute that was at stake; it was the very existence of Nephite society. Since everything was at stake, following the conventions and risking the possibility of losing all to the Lamanites simply would not do. Defending the existence of Nephite society required extraordinary measures, including Moroni's resort to stratagem.

Moroni's genius wasn't just in his technical innovations, but also in his ability to devise new stratagems—meaning devious maneuvers and tactics—to use against the Lamanites. The Lamanites eventually learned to expect them, but initially they were at a big disadvantage, perhaps assuming the Nephites would observe the conventions. Thus they supposed their numbers would give them the upper hand, as it always did under the old rules. However, Moroni was usually able to stay a step or two ahead of the Lamanites, devising new ruses to negate or neutralize Lamanite advantages when the old ones had worn out their usefulness.

However, there were some unforeseen consequences. By resorting to stratagem, Moroni may have changed warfare forever. The Lamanites eventually learned and adapted as well, adding stratagem to their battle menus. Once the rules had changed, it was nigh impossible to ever go back. This may be the real significance of the wars fought by Captain Moroni and the reason that they receive so much attention in the Book of Mormon. Like the Peloponnesian War, it was a turning point in Nephite history, leading to the eventual total destruction of the Nephite nation in Mormon's time, six hundred or so years after Captain Moroni. From this point on, the stakes were total domination, not temporary ritual victory through cyclic warfare.

Gaining Experience

Chapter 4: Battle of Sidon River Crossing

Moroni's first war occurred right after being appointed chief captain at the age of twenty-five. It was essentially a conventional war, though he began from the start to use stratagem. Many of the characteristics that would distinguish his career were displayed in his first battle, which makes it worth looking over and analyzing in depth. The Book of Mormon gives a detailed account of the events.

Sometime around the seventeenth year of the reign of the judges, a group of Nephites who were led by a man named Zoram[8] separated themselves from the Nephite people geographically and religiously (Alma 30:59). They began worshipping idols and adopted a strange method of praying (Alma 31:1, 12–18). They settled in a land called Antionum, which was nearly on the shore of the eastern sea south of Jershon but north of the wilderness (Alma 31:3). Jershon was a border state on the eastern seashore and the southern wilderness that separated the land of Nephi (occupied by the Lamanites) and the land of Zarahemla (occupied by the Nephites). The danger for the Nephites was that a Zoramite alliance with the Lamanites would increase the numbers of their enemies—which were already greater than the Nephites. More important, it'd give the Lamanites a salient north of the wilderness (Alma 31:4) that had until then provided a buffer for the Nephite armies, giving them enough time to mobilize against any

---

8. It's not clear if he was a descendant of the Zoram from Jerusalem.

Lamanite forays, a much-needed advantage. A beachhead north of the wilderness would eliminate this buffer and allow the Lamanites to attack practically without warning.

Nephite leaders recognized the great importance of eliminating this threat and sent missionaries to preach to the Zoramites and bring them back into the fold (Alma 31:5–6). The fact that the political separation by the Zoramites involved a change in worship practices and the solution devised by the Nephites was to send missionaries is a clear example of the inseparable nature of religion and politics in the Nephite world. Political legitimacy meant religious legitimacy. To change the political regime or politically secede, the rival leadership had to delegitimize the old religion too. This is likely a reason why Nephite dissenters were always attacking the religion. The system of government had been divinely sanctioned, and by attacking religion, dissenters sought to question the political system's inspired origins. Thus, to prevent political schisms and dissent, constant reaffirmation of the regimes' religious legitimacy was necessary.

The Nephite missionaries were successful among the Zoramite poor, but not so much among their elites (Alma 32:1–3). The Zoramite leadership mistakenly made an exclusionary religion, and because of the interrelated nature of religion and politics, this opened the door to Nephite missionaries. To prevent the erosion of their power, the Zoramite elite carried out a census of those who were in favor of the Nephite missionaries and expelled them from the community. The Book of Mormon indicates that there were many. They moved north into the neighboring land of Jershon, where the people of Ammon, or Ammonites (a Nephite group composed of exiled Lamanite converts), took them in.

While this allowed the Zoramite elite to maintain power, it also weakened their numbers, raising the fear among them that the large concentration of exiled Zoramites in the land next door could form an army and eventually overthrow the Zoramite elite. To prevent this, Zoramite leaders asked the Ammonites to break up this concentration of Zoramite exiles and expel them from Jershon. When the Ammonites refused and not only failed to expel them, but even fed, clothed, and gave these exiles land, the Zoramite elite threatened to attack the Ammonites. Having been weakened by the large reduction in their numbers and finding themselves in a rather vulnerable position north of wilderness, they then sought to form an alliance with the Lamanites and prepared for war with the Nephites (Alma 35:8–11).

Seeing these preparations, the Ammonites—who had taken an oath never to take up weapons of war—evacuated Jershon, ceding the region to the Nephite army (Alma 35:13). In order to make up for their inability to fight, the Ammonites gave a lot of their material substance to support the Nephite armies (Alma 43:13).

Meanwhile, the Lamanite armies who were under Zarahemnah occupied Antionum and integrated the remaining Zoramite dissidents into their forces. Interestingly, many Zoramites and Amalekites (another Nephite dissident group) were appointed to leadership posts among the Lamanite forces. According to the book's text, this was because they were of a more murderous disposition than the Lamanites were (Alma 43:6), as well as in recognition of their intimate knowledge of Nephite strengths, weaknesses, and geography. The Amalekites and Zoramites were largely noblemen, descendants of dissident Nephite priests and judges (Alma 43:13), and the average Amalekite or Zoramite may have been more educated than the average Lamanite and thus better candidates for officer positions.

Most of the Nephite dissidents then and in the future would be frustrated mid-level elites—those who had ambitions blocked by the Nephite social and religious higher-ups. In many studies of insurgency and rebellion, it should be noted that it's precisely when such groups are excluded from power that insurgency and revolution commonly occur. This isn't meant to indicate sympathy for or value judgments on the frustrated dissident causes in the Book of Mormon, but rather it's an attempt to offer a logical explanation as to why things happened the way they did.

The Lamanites may have wanted to mobilize and overwhelm the Nephites in Jershon, but the Nephites had mobilized more quickly because they were operating along interior lines[9] and were prepared for the oncoming Lamanites.

Among the preparations that Moroni instituted was the universal issue of protective armor, apparently for the first time in the Book of Mormon. Captain Moroni faced the problem of defeating a vastly superior force with his own force that was half its size. His solution was to equip all of his men with a new type of armor (as described earlier in this book) in an attempt to even the odds, making his men superior to their opponents.

When the Lamanites saw this, they sought to gain the advantage by marching into the wilderness, hoping to attack the Nephites at an unexpected location of their choosing (Alma 43:22). They may have thought that, unencumbered by armor, they'd out-march the Nephite army and launch an attack before the Nephites could prepare.

However, Moroni sent spies (or scouts) to find the Lamanite army and also sent messengers to the prophets to ask for divine guidance. From the prophets, he learned the general but not specific location the Lamanites were going to attempt to attack (Alma 43:24). From the scouts, he probably narrowed the options down further. Moroni immediately marched with his armies to Manti, arriving ahead of the Lamanites. He was able to out-march the Lamanite armies for several reasons. First, he received timely information from the prophets and his scouts. Second, while encumbered by armor, his men marched along interior lines through developed flatlands and paved roads. In contrast, the Lamanites marched along exterior lines, going into the wilderness, which was no doubt difficult and far less developed terrain.

---

9. In military terminology, *interior lines* are the lines within a defensive perimeter. By contrast, the attackers moving outside the defensive perimeter move on *exterior lines*. Interior lines are almost always shorter and more developed. Exterior lines are often longer and less developed. The attackers usually take much longer and experience more difficulty moving from one place to another. As a consequence, defenders have the advantage of being able to quickly move their forces to reinforce the point of attack, whereas attackers have to spend far longer moving their forces from one point of attack to another. This is one reason attackers attempt to mass at least twice as many forces as defenders at the point of attack. This also contributes to the amount of time required to move from one point to another.

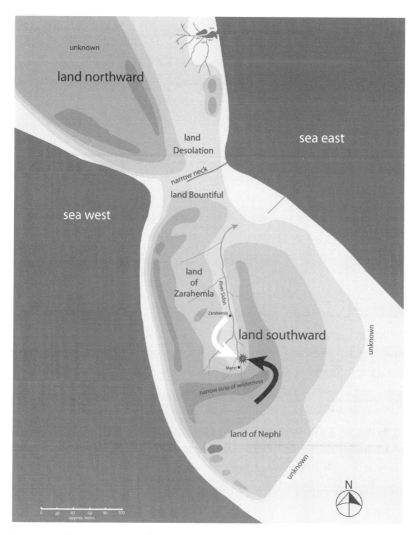

Lamanite Campaign. Based on *Mormon's Map*. Courtesy of John L. Sorenson (Provo, Utah: Farms, 2000).

To enter the Nephite lands, the Lamanites had to cross the Sidon River. Apparently the best crossing for an army was through a narrow valley running east and west, split by the river. The dominant hill over this valley was called Riplah; a trade route or well-worn trail may have crossed from the northeast into the valley to the river crossing.[10]

10. John L. Sorenson, *An Ancient American Setting for the Book of Mormon* (Salt Lake City: Deseret Book, 1996), 255.

Moroni then used logic and spies to determine the route that the enemies would use and resolved to set up an ambush. This isn't the first time Nephite forces ambushed their Lamanite foes. Limhi, King Noah's son, successfully executed an ambush when his outnumbered forces had faced overwhelming odds (Mosiah 20:8–9).

Captain Moroni performed a risky maneuver, one not generally recommended for a commander of an outnumbered force. He divided his men, placing half of his troops under the reliable and steady Lehi on the east side of the river while the remainder was positioned on the west side of the river under his command (Alma 43:31–33). Both forces concealed themselves in the densely vegetated hills of the valley. The traditional combat tactics in such a situation would've been to mass all of the forces on the west side and have a head-on battle to prevent the enemy from crossing. However, Captain Moroni knew the sheer mass of the Lamanite army would probably overwhelm his forces, so he devised a battle plan that relied on the element of surprise, hoping to neutralize the Lamanites' advantage in numbers.

Captain Moroni likely planned for his forces to remain undetected until the Lamanites were partly across the river, at which time he would hit them from both sides, catching them at their most vulnerable—in the water. There, the Nephites would be able to inflict heavy casualties and quickly gain the upper hand before the Lamanites could organize a defense or counterattack, boxing them in the river, where they would be at the mercy of the Nephite armies. As long as the Lamanite army could be kept in the river or on the banks, the Nephites could rain down arrows and stones from the valley walls and destroy them at will. To ensure the success of the battle, Captain Moroni placed spies on all sides of the valley so that last-minute adjustments could be made according to the observed size, direction, and speed of the Lamanite forces, also ensuring that the trap would not be sprung too early (Alma 43:28).

When word of the Lamanite approach reached Captain Moroni, he deployed his army, sending Lehi's forces to concealed positions on Riplah Hill. Lehi's forces were divided between the eastern and southern slopes, probably slightly to the east. Captain Moroni's forces were concealed in the west part of the valley across the Sidon River and divided into two groups: one that was positioned along the northern ridges lining the valley, and the other on the southern ridges (Alma 43:31–34, 41–42).

The Lamanites approached the crossing along the expected route, probably traveling on a well-known road, path, or trade route. Any other route would have made it difficult for the Nephites to know where on the southern slope of the hill to set up and stay concealed. Apparently the Lamanites were not all that security conscious, which indicates they believed that their numbers and speed gave them the advantage of surprise and that the Nephites were not aware of where they were. The Lamanite leaders were more concerned about speed than security, hoping to take Manti before the Nephite armies could react, allowing them to get between the Nephite armies—believed to be in Jershon—and the capital of the land, Zarahemla.

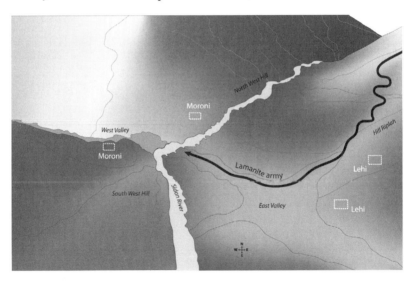

An aerial view of the Battle of Sidon River Crossing—phase 1.

The Lamanites started up the northern slope of Riplah Hill and reached the crest. They were well on their way down the southern slope, and in all probability some of them had started crossing the river, when the battle started prematurely. Either Captain Lehi gave the order to attack too soon, overzealous Nephites soldiers couldn't wait, or the Lamanites spotted some Nephite soldiers despite their efforts to stay concealed. At any rate, the battle started (Alma 43:35).

The Lamanites were surprised and probably hesitated. Lehi would have taken advantage of this hesitation to attack aggressively, making up for the fact that the battle started earlier than planned. He pressed home the attack by ordering his forces on the eastern slope of the hill to strike the Lamanites from the rear while his armies on the southern slope struck the Lamanites' left flank. The onslaught caused disorganization and confusion, but the Lamanites managed to overcome the surprise and face the threat. However, the Nephites body armor gave them an effective advantage and Lamanites fell with nearly every stroke and thrust of the Nephite weapons, while Nephites fell irregularly. This invulnerability had a demoralizing effect. Adding to the confusion of having to turn an entire army to face an ambush, the sheer inertia the attacking Nephites attained as they attacked downhill proved too much for the Lamanites (Alma 43:34–38).

An aerial view of the Battle of Sidon River Crossing—phase 2.

Probably thinking this to be the main Nephite force, the Lamanite leaders reasoned that disengaging most of their numbers—except a rearguard—and rapidly crossing the river could enable them to escape from the ambush and resume their march. This, however, became their undoing. Had they fought Lehi's forces first, they probably could have cut their way through and destroyed the Nephites, regardless of their body armor, and then either escaped or faced Moroni's troops on more advantageous footing. Instead, they made the fateful choice to disengage and turn toward the river. Lehi's forces drove the Lamanites' rearguard down into the river and then, according to Moroni's plan, stopped on the river bank (Alma 43:39–40).

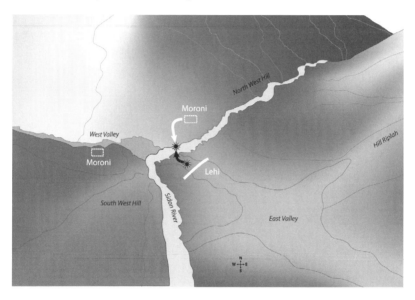

An aerial view of the Battle of Sidon River Crossing—phase 3

As the Lamanites reached the western bank of the river, Moroni's forces attacked from the north ridge across the valley. The battle then developed exactly according to Moroni's plan. The Lamanite choice to cross instead of contending with Lehi's force meant Moroni's forces cut off their escape to the west and north, and Lehi cut off their retreat. They still weren't trapped and thus tried to bypass Moroni by turning southward. However, Moroni had anticipated this move and concealed another force along the southern ridge of the valley. The Lamanites were then entirely boxed in (Alma 43:41–42). However, the Lamanites, in battling Lehi's force early along the slopes of Riplah Hill, had overcome their initial shock from the ambush and the Nephites' advantage in armor. They realized the potential impact of their tremendous numerical advantage, even against armor. The

Lamanites adapted and began effectively using their great advantage in numbers and mobility to attack—being less weighed down without the thick clothing and hard plates of the Nephites. The account states the Lamanites began to fight like dragons to the point that they split many of the Nephites' head plates in two, pierced the breastplates, and cut off numerous arms (Alma 43:43–44).

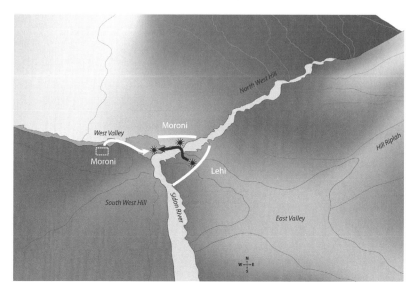

An aerial view of the Battle of Sidon River Crossing—phase 4.

The Nephites, who had up to that point enjoyed a tremendous advantage in morale because of their protective armor and superior tactics, began to show signs of giving way because their armor was not protecting them as much as it had initially. Though surrounding the Lamanites, their lines were comparatively thin and being stretched rapidly. The Nephites nearly broke ranks and fled from the ferocity of their enemies. However, Captain Moroni, realizing that his men's spirits were failing, reminded the Nephites of their strategic situation, what they were fighting for, and the consequences if they lost. How he did this isn't clear; perhaps he amplified his voice through some device, ran up and down his lines himself, or wrote messages and sent runners. According to the account, he inspired the Nephites to call upon the Lord with one voice, enough to reinvigorate them to respond to the Lamanites' energy with equal fury (Alma 43:48–50). The Lamanite spirits flagged as their overwhelming numbers proved insufficient and the tide of the battle turned against them. Having lost their final opportunity to break the Nephites encirclement, the Lamanites were struck with terror as they realized that their situation was hopeless and that they were going to die. Their morale evaporated (Alma 43:50).

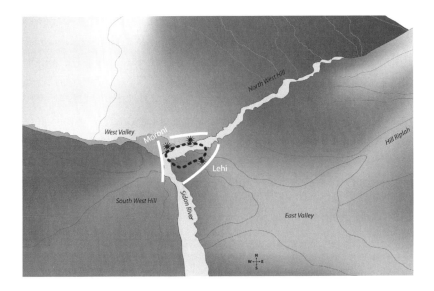

An aerial view of the Battle of Sidon River Crossing—phase 5.

Captain Moroni could've allowed the slaughter to continue, but being a leader who did not delight in bloodshed, he instead ordered his men to cease the killing and withdraw a pace (Alma 43:54). Moroni then went forward to talk to the Lamanite battle leader, Zarahemnah, demanding that the Lamanites surrender all of their weapons and take an oath that they would never come to war against the Nephites again (Alma 44:1–7). Zarahemnah was willing to give up the weapons, but he wouldn't make the oath, his reasoning being that it was an oath his men and their future children would break (Alma 44:8). Apparently an oath in this ancient culture was an incredibly serious affair, binding even subsequent generations.

When Captain Moroni heard the answer, he called Zarahemnah's bluff and returned to Zarahemnah his weapons. And to emphasize his determination, Moroni swore his own oath: "As the Lord liveth," if the Lamanites didn't take the oath, the Nephites would slaughter all of them (Alma 44:10–11).

This so enraged Zarahemnah that he charged Moroni, hoping to kill him. However, one of Captain Moroni's soldiers—probably an officer or bodyguard—leapt forward and knocked Zarahemnah's sword out of his hand. It isn't clear whether the same blow cut off the Lamanite leader's scalp or whether the Nephite soldier subsequently and deliberately cut off Zarahemnah's scalp. Regardless of which one it was, Zarahemnah's scalp was removed. He was dragged back, bleeding, by his own men.

The Nephite scalper-soldier then stepped forward and conducted a remarkably macabre piece of psychological warfare. He placed the scalp on the end of his sword and held it up for all the Lamanites to see, after which he quite dramatically dropped it onto the ground. His message was simple: This represented the Lamanites who would fall to the ground—like the scalp—unless they agreed to the oath Moroni required of them (Alma 44:12–14).

Many of the Lamanites were so horrified that they came forward and took the oath, which infuriated others—including the scalped and humiliated Zarahemnah. Those Lamanites who made the oath were allowed by the Nephites to depart. After their departure, the battle was renewed (Alma 44:15–16), but the psychological effect of the scalp and the deserters took its toll and drained away the Lamanites' will to keep fighting. Moreover, they were more boxed in than ever, weakened by desertion, demoralized, and truly had nowhere to turn. The slaughter was immense. Zarahemnah finally gave in and cried out that he would take the oath rather than lose his life. Captain Moroni promptly ordered that the killing stop once again (Alma 44:17–20). Apparently Zarahemnah kept his oath, as he is never heard of again in Mormon's account.

Thus ended Moroni's first battle as chief captain. In this battle, he showed the first flashes of military genius that would make him great: technical and tactical innovation and reliance on divine inspiration—all combined with intelligence, cunning, nerve, aggressiveness, personal courage, leadership, passion, and true mercy. The great commander had begun a promising career, one that would define his life and a good chunk of the book of Alma.

Battles of Experience

Chapter 5: The Great War

At the end of Alma 45, Helaman and his brethren went throughout the land of the Nephites in order to reestablish the Church and appoint new priests and teachers to lead the local churches. This is another example of the fused nature of church and politics, as the account discusses how this missionary effort resulted in dissension within the Church.

A group coalesced in opposition to the priests and teachers who had been appointed by Helaman, composed of wealthy and ambitious lower judges seeking power (Alma 45:23–24; 46:4). This group felt that having to submit to religious authority interfered with their political ambitions. So clearly, in Nephite society, religious dissent was equivalent to political dissent. Their animosity toward Helaman was such that they conspired to slay Helaman and the missionaries (Alma 46:2). The Church interfered with their political agenda.

An important element in coming to understand the link between resistance to the Church and political dissension in Nephite society seems to have been related to lineage. Lineage determined leadership: the priests, kings, and chief judges were all direct descendants of Nephi. Other lineages didn't seem to share this status, a fact that helps make sense of the continual dissension in the larger Nephite civilization. This society was a mixed group, from the beginning composed of Lehi's children, Zoram, some of Ishmael's daughters, and possibly some of Ishmael's sons. When this group was forced to leave the land of Nephi or face extinction, it traveled until finding the people of Zarahemla, who had also emigrated from Palestine under the leadership of Mulek, a son of Zedekiah, king of Judah.

The two societies then united, and Mosiah, the Nephite leader, was appointed king, probably because the Nephites had preserved records and maintained the religion (Omni 1:14–19), even though the people of Zarahemla outnumbered the people of Nephi (Mosiah 25:2). It is probable that the people of Zarahemla were also a composite group, having absorbed some of the survivors of the Jaredites.

This set up at least four separate claims on leadership, producing continual conflict within the overall civilization. A smaller minority—the literal descendants of Nephi—ruled over several different ethnic groups, the latter being far greater in number than the ethnic Nephites. The legitimacy of this arrangement was based on religious grounds, a fact that required religious justification and validation, without which the claim to the government was also illegitimate. Second in line were the descendants of Mulek, son of King Zedekiah, ruler of Jerusalem around 600 BC. Third, the possible descendents of Coriantumr, an even more ancient line of Jaredites kings that tracked their lineage back to the tower of Babel. Both of these royal lineages existed in the subordinate majority with latent aspirations to regain their thrones or the right of rule, though none was able to do so without significantly altering the existing order.

Fourth in importance were the descendants of Zoram, who had no royal blood but had been instrumental in providing the brass plates—the source of the law in Nephite society. Without the brass plates, the Nephite claim to authority was weak, and without Zoram, the Nephites would have never obtained the brass plates. The glue that held this system together was the Nephites' ability to convince everyone that the system of government was divinely mandated and thus legitimate. However, without the religious justification, the political order could not stand. The political arrangement worked most of the time, as the Nephites seemed to be pretty fair-minded and conscience rulers, with a few notable exceptions. When problems arose because of wickedness or injustice, the competing claims were always used as banners to mobilize contending sides. These issues and perceived injustices remained close enough to the surface that almost any situation could quickly descend into political conflict and war.

Amalickiah was a descendant of Zoram, a lineage that was not usually associated with leadership, yet he aspired to be king (Alma 54:23). The justification for war, according to his brother Ammoron, was that the ancestors of the Nephites stole their ancestors' right to rule (Alma 54:17–18). It's probable that Ammoron was using the Lamanites' argument to bolster his case, speaking from his assumed kingship in the Lamanite society. However, in a subsequent verse, he discusses his Zoramite lineage and the wrongs that the Nephite people purportedly inflicted on Zoram as well (Alma 54:23–24). Perhaps because of Zoram's important role in the acquisition of the brass plates—one of the Nephites' major sources of power—and subsequent lack of a leadership role made the descendants of Zoram feel they had been wronged.

The fact is that Lamanite, Zoramite, Zarahemlite, or Jaredite family groups could've all made similar claims against the Nephites. In this context, religion was perceived as being the medium through which the Nephites had gained and maintained their domination over a diverse group of people. The perception was probably best expressed by the religious dissenter Korihor, who said that the Nephite religion kept the people in bondage, so they dared not enjoy their rights and privileges, particularly the enjoyment of their material wealth. Instead, he purported that the leaders, both religious and governmental, would glut themselves with the labor of the people (Alma 30:24–28). Thus, the first step in a political overthrow of the Nephite government was to overthrow the religion. Captain Moroni knew that as a means of taking over the government, Amalickiah sought to destroy their religion as well (Alma 46:18).

However, most people didn't buy into Amalickiah's bid for the kingdom, and he was unable to mobilize enough followers to launch a successful internal war. Consequently, he had to flee to the Lamanite lands, where he used flattery, deception, appeals to vanity, poison, assassination, and seduction to gain control of the Lamanite armies first and then the Lamanite kingdom by murdering the king and seducing the king's widow. Most Lamanites were extremely reluctant to go to war with the Nephites again, so Amalickiah hired a number of prop-agandists to incite the Lamanites, day and night, to anger against the Nephites. Once the Lamanites were sufficiently agitated, it was easy for him to mobilize an army and order it to march toward the Nephite lands (Alma 48:1–6). This method of mobilizing people to war through propagandists is reminiscent of the similar technique employed by the Nazis to infuse Germans with hatred toward Jews, Slavs, and all "untermensch,"[11] and to believe in the vital necessity of going to war to establish the Third Reich. For that matter, these techniques—today called *psychological operations*—are used to some degree by all warring countries to incite patriotic fervor and gain support for military campaigns.

Meanwhile, Captain Moroni hadn't been idle. Aware of what was going on, probably through his spies, he prepared for battle. The Lamanites had adopted body armor just like that used previously by the Nephites, so Captain Moroni developed his next innovation: dirt and timber fortifications. While Amalickiah mobilized the Lamanites, Captain Moroni also mobilized his people to build new fortifications around every city. He didn't have to wait long to test them in battle (Alma 48:7–9).

The Battle of the City of Noah

The first battle that involved the new fortifications occurred in the latter part of the year 72 BC. The Lamanites marched through the wilderness to attack the city of Ammonihah, a city they had completely destroyed only a few years earlier in a previous war. This city was in the northwest, east of a mountain range that stabbed north into Nephite lands from Lamanite lands and thus could be used as a concealed invasion route.

The Nephites, having been invaded once along this route, had built exceedingly strong fortifications around Ammonihah, so when the Lamanite military leaders saw the city and its new fortifications, they didn't dare attack. Instead, they decided to march back through the wilderness to another traditionally weak Nephite city: the city of Noah. Before they reached this city, they swore an oath that they would attack it no matter what. When they reached the city of Noah, however, it was as well fortified as the city of Ammonihah and commanded by the Lamanites' old nemesis, Captain Lehi. Lehi's presence caused them to hesitate (Alma 49:17), but since they had sworn an oath, they dared

---

11. Literally translated as "under men," essentially sub-humans.

not turn back and break it. Note again the absolutely unbreakable nature of oaths. These military leaders felt it was more important to honor their oath than it was to spare their own lives and those of their men.

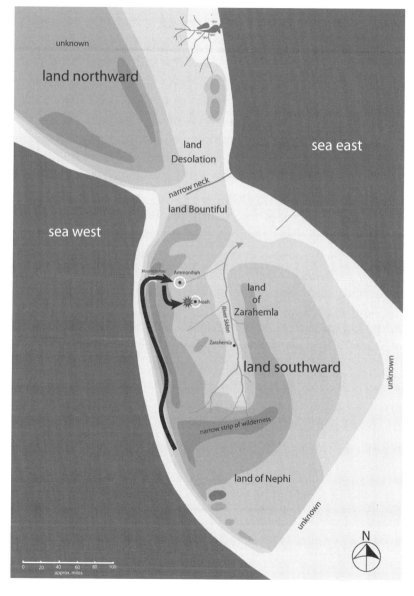

First Lamanite Campaign: Battle of Noah. Based on *Mormon's Map*. Courtesy of John L. Sorenson (Provo: Farms, 2000).

The Lamanites surveyed the Nephite fortifications and noticed the only place that was not intensely fortified was the main entrance, deceptively enticing because it was protected by a few men in the gap. To the Lamanites, it seemed that they had found the weakness in the Nephite's defensive system where they could take advantage of their vastly superior numbers by merely running enough men through the gap. If this could be done successfully, they could overwhelm the few defenders at this location, breach the fortifications, and take the city. However, this was a serious error on their part. Several waves of men were sent to assault the main entrance, but each of these assaults were completely routed (Alma 49:21). As the men descended into the ditch, they were flailed by a multitude of rocks and arrows from the cleverly sighted towers dominating the ditch. There was hardly any place in the ditch safe from these missiles, except the far side closest to the city where the angle was too awkward for the majority of the arrows and stones to hit consistently. However, with the number of projectiles flying through the air, even this sanctuary was not safe.

From the description in the account, it would seem that most of the Lamanites never even made it across. The majority may not have been killed there, but almost all were surely wounded. Those that managed to get to the far side of the ditch and were brave enough to climb out to approach the entrance found themselves even more exposed to the projectiles launched from the towers. The ditch wall was steep, so anyone attempting to climb it would've been delayed and thus exposed for a time as they attempted to extricate themselves. However, once out of the ditch, the nightmare only got worse. Some relative protection could be found by hugging the large mounds of dirt, but the Lamanites couldn't get close with the Nephites right on top of them.

The only way to get close was to charge down the entrance that, because of its narrowness, only permitted a few men to move through it at a time. Along this narrow corridor, the attackers stacked up and were exposed to the slings and arrows of men in the towers on either flank, as well as archers and stone throwers behind the line of men waiting for them at the entrance itself. The Lamanites who fell became obstacles to the men behind them, further narrowing the gap, slowing down the advance, and exposing those foolish enough to continue trying to get past the defenders' stones and arrows. By the time the few attackers reached the entrance, they were tired and demoralized. Most men had probably already suffered multiple hits from arrows and stones and if not wounded were severely battered, their armor bristling like porcupines with shafts. They were easily cut down with little effort by the fresh Nephite soldiers stationed at the entrance gap.

The Lamanites then tried to counter the Nephite archers and rock throwers by bringing up their own archers. However, in order to get within range, the Lamanite archers had to expose themselves to the Nephite archers and rock throwers, who had the advantage of fortified positions and height. Height gave several advantages to the Nephite defenders. First, the Nephites could fire directly at targets of their own choosing while the Lamanites had to fire indirectly, a much more difficult task. Second, it required less muscle power to pull on the bow to achieve the same result, so for the same pull, the Nephites could shoot further and with more hitting power. Third, the Nephites had a much better view of their targets than the Lamanites. These advantages meant that before the Lamanite archers could get within range, they were already being targeted and hit by the Nephite archers. Moreover, the Lamanites were totally exposed while the Nephite archers enjoyed the protection of their fortified towers. Only an occasional Lamanite arrow penetrated, and most of these were deflected by the Nephite body armor. However, probably because of the indirect angle, some arrows managed to penetrate and strike the Nephite archers' legs. According to the account, because the Nephite soldiers' legs were not armored, many received severe wounds to their lower limbs (Alma 49:24).

The battle was a horrible scene of carnage. Despite the tendency of Book of Mormon readers to be pro-Nephite, readers can really only feel pity for the dazed, confused, yet brave Lamanite soldiers as wave after wave kept pouring into that awful ditch. After only a short period of time, the bottom of the ditch was filled with the bodies of the dead and wounded, whose moans and screams filled the subsequent waves with a choking sense of fear (Alma 49:22). Inside the ditch, pelted by the rain of stones and arrows, military cohesion broke down and many of the Lamanite wounded would have been trampled to death as their comrades attempted to escape the stones and arrows. As the gore and bodies piled up, each successive wave was forced to slip and slide on the bodies of their fellows as they attempted to avoid the rain of death from above and make it across the ditch. Those that did found no comfort as their unwounded officers screamed and cursed at the men, pushing their men to climb the ditch to attack the entrance. The consequences of this have already been discussed and it is clear that most never made it to the narrow entrance, though several attempts were made. The account mentions that they were driven back from time to time (Alma 49:21). A few lucky ones withdrew from the entrance gap, some to the relative safety of the edge of the mound. As they were still exposed to stones and arrows, they instinctively began to dig into the dirt to give them more cover. The Nephite archers ignored these men because they were not posing a threat at the time.

The instinctive digging for cover by those who had reached the mound wall inspired the Lamanites to try a new tactic; they began trying to fill in the ditch. However, instead of doing so at the entrance, they would likely have made an attempt at a new location on the flank (Alma 49:22). Perhaps they tried to hold the Nephites' attention at the entrance during this effort. In this, they hoped the Nephites wouldn't notice until it was too late. If they could get enough men across the ditch and to the mound, they would pull down the wall and fill up the ditch. The deeper they dug into the mound, the more they would also be protected from Nephite rocks and arrows. Filling in the ditch would accomplish two things: allow the Lamanites to cross the ditch quickly—exposing them for less time to the Nephite projectiles   and create another gap in the defenses that would force the Nephites to divide their forces to deal with the new threat. The Lamanites would then have a more equal advantage, and in the process protect the archers and sling throwers brought up behind the scrapes.

But the Nephites weren't fooled. At great cost, the Lamanites sent forces across the ditch at one or more points to the edge of the mound to pull down the dirt and fill in the ditch. It's obvious that the Nephite archer towers were sighted to be mutually supporting. Where the slings and arrows of one tower couldn't hit the Lamanites, those of its neighbor could. Furthermore, as the Lamanites carried the dirt to the edge of the ditch, they were immediately attacked. In this manner, the ditches began to be filled, not with dirt but with the dead Lamanite soldiers (Alma 49:22). The new Lamanite tactic might have actually worked had they persisted long enough. However, they had already suffered great casualties from the first waves at the entrance and, in the end, all of the Lamanite leaders were killed. As mentioned previously, they preferred to die in combat rather than break their oaths.

Leaderless, the Lamanite soldiers' morale shattered (Alma 49:25). Most of the leaders were Amalekites, Zoramites, and other Nephite dissenters. Because the Lamanite conscripts had much less personal incentive to fight, they fled into the wilderness and headed back to the land of Nephi (Alma 49:25). The battle cost the Lamanites well over a thousand soldiers (Alma 49:23). The Nephites suffered no dead and only fifty wounded. Most of these were suffered at the main entrance and were wounds on the men's unprotected legs (Alma 49:24). This seems to indicate that the Lamanites never got close enough for any hand-to-hand combat. Probably all of the wounds were caused by arrows and slings—and maybe an odd spear or two (Alma 49:19). It was a great Nephite victory. However, it wouldn't last. Their enemies would learn, adapt, and make new attempts.

Chapter 6: The Introduction of Strategic Thinking

Amalickiah waited five years before attacking again, and in the meantime both peoples prepared for war. Amalickiah apparently waited to make an overt attack until an internal rebellion in the Nephite government broke out in civil war. Though the account does not say, this rebellion may have been deliberately fomented by Amalickiah through secret contact and promises to his sympathizers still in the land of Zarahemla. Ensuring this rebellion got off the ground may have delayed Amalickiah's second effort for five years, as his overt strategy was to strike the Nephites while they were distracted by domestic problems. He had prepared a huge army and began a campaign to take control of the lands northeast of the seashore, specifically Moroni and Bountiful. Because the creation of this huge army would've required considerable time and effort during the five-year interlude, this lends stronger credence to the idea that the internal Nephite rebellion was more than just a coincidence.

The land of Bountiful was the final objective of this campaign, as gaining control of Bountiful gave the possessor access to the narrow pass that led into the land northward. If the Lamanites controlled this pass, they could surround the Nephites with hostile forces to the south, east, and north. The Nephites would've been surrounded, with their backs to the west sea. If the Nephite dissenters managed to take control of Zarahemla to the southwest, the remaining Nephites would've been trapped between Zarahemla and Bountiful within the Sidon River valley.

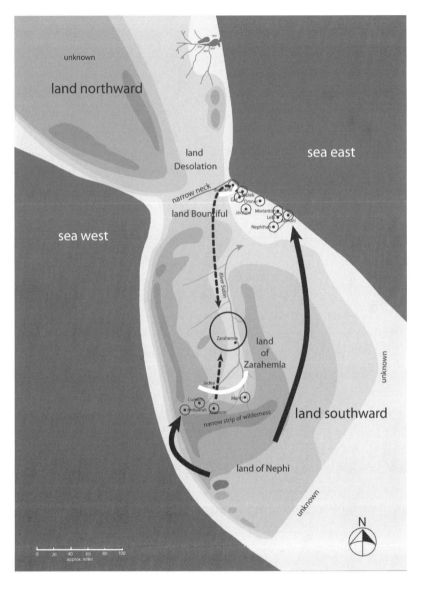

Second Lamanite Campaign: Pincers and Internal Rebellion. Based on *Mormon's Map*. Courtesy of John L. Sorenson (Provo: Farms, 2000).

The Lamanite strategy nearly worked, but the Nephites were aware of the critical vulnerability in the east, and in the interim between the Lamanite attack on Noah and Amalickiah's second campaign, they had taken measures to strengthen their position there.

There were apparently a number of Lamanites—perhaps nomadic groups or frontier farmers—who had crept into the wilderness to the east of the river Sidon but north of recognized Lamanite lands. This occupation formed a dangerous salient that could serve as a potential jumping-off point for an army attempting to attack the heart of the Nephite lands: the Sidon River Valley. Also, it potentially divided and separated the Nephite defenses, a weakness that Moroni wanted to eliminate by straightening and consolidating the Nephite defensive line, which explains why the account emphasizes the defense of a straight line (Alma 50:8). Moroni had his armies drive these hapless Lamanites south into Lamanite lands (Alma 50:7), thus eliminating a potential source of logistics, recruits, and intelligence for the Lamanite armies. And to make sure they didn't come back, he resettled those lands with Nephites, an early form of ethnic cleansing (Alma 50:9), a common measure applied in ancient warfare. Today, this would be strenuously condemned as an abuse of human rights, but Mormon apparently thought nothing of it and made no apologies. Finally, Moroni built a number of additional fortress cities (Alma 50:13–15), including Moroni (no doubt named after him), Nephihah, and Lehi (probably named after Captain Lehi).

These efforts may show how warfare was changing in the Nephite society. A subtle but clear escalation and shift in Nephite-Lamanite military thinking was steadily occurring. Prior to this, war could've been seen as a single-battle affair focused on single decisive events and individual cities. The Lamanite destruction of Ammonihah, the Battle of the Sidon River Crossing, and even the more recent Battle of Noah were single battle affairs dealing with conquering and defending in a single event, the old system of war. Now the Lamanites and Moroni had begun thinking strategically in increasingly sophisticated ways. The Lamanite strategic approach was described above. Moroni's first step toward strategy had been to strengthen the fortifications and defenses of multiple cities. While this was indeed strategic in the sense of across-the-board improvement, in battle each city essentially stood alone. With the new effort, Moroni shows he was thinking at a higher strategic level. By straightening the Nephite defensive line and resettling inhabitants and building new fortified cities, he was creating a nationally integrated defensive system.

The reason the internal rebellion of Morianton—which you might wonder why Mormon included it in the account, as it seems like a distracting side story to the casual reader—was so critical was because it threatened to unhinge this defensive system Moroni had so carefully developed. Morianton sought to dissent from the Nephites and flee to the land northward of the narrow pass, past the land of Bountiful. Having potential enemies to the north that could make alliances with the Lamanites to the south and thus sandwich the Nephites in between them was completely unacceptable. This is why Moroni moved so quickly to suppress Morianton and keep his strategic defensive system intact (Alma 50:25–36).

However, the Nephite preparations were almost all for naught, because when Amalickiah and his army renewed their attack, Nephite resources were largely being dedicated to the internal war (Alma 51:22). Without the integrated Nephite defensive system, perhaps the Lamanites would have been victorious, as they were also now thinking strategically. Their armies, under the direct command of Amalickiah, had developed new siege tactics. These are not described, but they are inferred as they were able to take control of the eastern cities of Moroni, Nephihah, Lehi, Morianton, Omner, Gid, and Mulek—but not the key city of Bountiful, which guarded the northern pass (Alma 51:23–31). The Nephite defensive system had barely succeeded in stopping the Lamanites strategic success.

While the record doesn't mention it directly, there is subsequent information in Helaman's epistles to Captain Moroni indicating that the Lamanites launched a simultaneous strike along the west coast. He mentions in an offhand manner that several Nephite cities in this area were already occupied by the Lamanites. From this, it can be deduced that the Lamanite strategy consisted of a two-pronged pincer attack. The main effort under Amalickiah sought to close off the Nephite escape valve to the north. The effort in the southwest was probably to attack toward Zarahemla in an effort to link up with the Nephite dissenters, who were known as "king men." This way, the remaining Nephites would be caught in the Sidon River valley between two Lamanite armies. Either the northeast hook or the southwest one could then advance into the valley to smash the Nephite armies between two great Lamanite forces. This sound military strategy came much closer to success than the account seems to admit.

Both the northeastern and southwestern drives had great successes until the Nephites finally managed to end their internal strife. By the twenty-sixth year of the reign of the judges, when Helaman led his two thousand warriors to fight on the western front, the Lamanites in the southwest had won possession of the land and cities of Manti, Zeezrom, Cumeni, and Antiparah (Alma 56:14). The land of Manti was the Nephite holding furthest to the south along the Sidon River (Alma 16:6). Antiparah, according to Sorenson, was probably located in a narrow valley pass between the Sidon River valley and the west coast.[12] This narrow valley pass bordered both the land of Manti and the land of Judea, occupied by the Nephite army led by Antipus. This force was the only thing that stood between the Lamanites and Zarahemla.

The Antiparah Maneuver

Antipus and his army were battered and desperate. They had been conducting a grinding campaign in the southwest, where they had been systematically defeated and driven out of a number of cities. The Lamanites had captured the crucial mountain fortress of Antiparah and subsequently taken Manti. Only Antipus and his demoralized army in Judea stood in the way of the Lamanites and the land of Zarahemla, and the city of Judea was vulnerable. Helaman and his two thousand young reinforcements—known as "stripling warriors"— arrived at a critical time in the twenty-sixth year. These reinforcements were sufficient in number to cause the Lamanites to stop their drive and to consolidate the lands they had taken, rebuild their fortifications, and await reinforcements and provisions (Alma 56:18–20). Both sides dedicated the rest of that year to recuperating and rebuilding.

Antipus and his commanders analyzed their situation. They knew that even with Helaman's reinforcements, their position at Judea was precarious. The city could be bypassed. Cities to the north could be taken because they lacked adequate garrisons and fortifications. If the Lamanites could pass Judea without detection, they could take a lot of territory before the Nephites could react. To make sure this didn't happen, the Nephite army developed a plan to trap the Lamanite forces,

---

12. John L. Sorenson, *An Ancient American Setting for the Book of Mormon* (Salt Lake City: Deseret Book, 1996), 257–58.

posting spies all around to provide Antipus with adequate warning so that a Nephite army could march and strike the Lamanites in the rear just as they started to attack one of the cities further north.

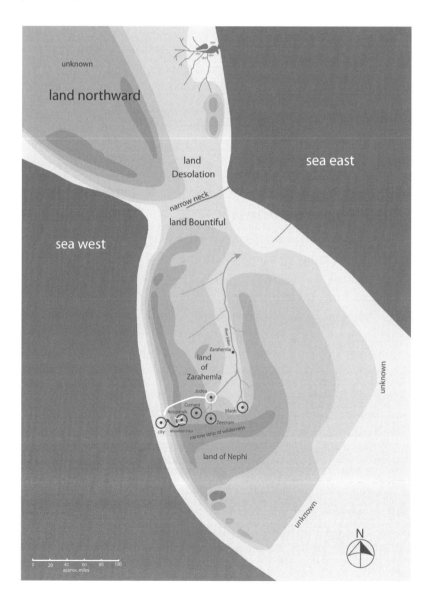

The Antiparah Maneuver, Move 1. Based on *Mormon's Map*. Courtesy of John L. Sorenson (Provo: Farms, 2000).

The timing of the Nephite attack was critical to the success of the plan, because by doing this, Antipus would effectively trap the Lamanite forces between the walls of the defending city and his army. However, the Lamanites were wary of Nephite capabilities and remained in their conquered cities (Alma 56:21–26). Even as static forces, the Lamanite armies were a significant threat, especially to the land of Zarahemla. The Nephite commanders believed it was only a matter of time before the Lamanites received additional support and renewed their offensive operations. Before this could happen, the Nephites had to find a way to draw the Lamanites out of the cities and fight them in the open, where they felt they could gain the advantage.

The linchpin in the Lamanite defensive network was the city of Antiparah. It guarded the mountain pass between the western shore and the land of Manti. If the city could be taken and the pass sealed off, then the only route available to the Lamanites into the heart of Nephite territory would be through a northern march along the coast, then across the wilderness, and down to the cities of Ammonihah and Noah. This was the same route the Lamanites had used initially, which had ended in the disaster at the city of Noah.

However, the Nephites weren't strong enough to besiege the city, so they reasoned that the best way to take it back was to somehow draw the garrison out and destroy it on a more equal footing. The Nephites spent five months preparing their plan to lure the garrison out of Antiparah, readying ten thousand troops to carry out their plan. The Nephites made invitations to the garrison to fight in the open, but the Lamanites refused and ignored other attempts to draw them out.

Patiently watching the enemy, the opportunity finally came. The Nephites noticed that in the early part of the twenty-seventh year, the Lamanites reacted nervously when the Nephites received supplies, sending out forces to attempt to intercept the supply columns. The Nephites decided that they would use this Lamanite uneasiness as the means to draw them into a trap (Alma 56:30). In the seventh month of the twenty-seventh year, Helaman and his two thousand young men were sent to a city beyond the pass guarded by Antiparah on the western seashore. They disguised themselves as a logistical column. When the Lamanite garrison at Antiparah saw this column, they dutifully left the city and pursued it. As the account just finished emphasizing their refusal to come out of the city, what would suddenly cause the Lamanites to abandon caution to the wind and fall for this seemingly simple ruse?

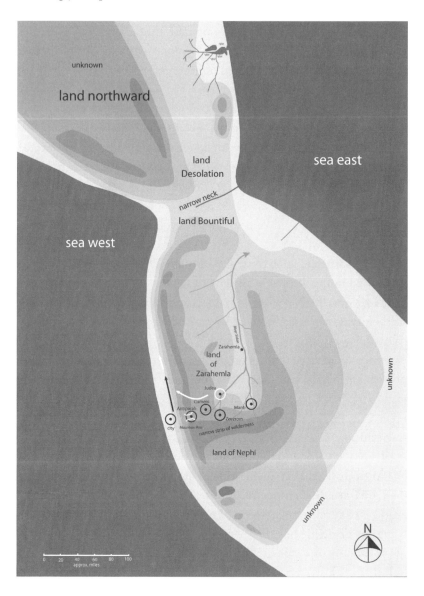

The Antiparah Maneuver, Move 2. Based on *Mormon's Map.* Courtesy of John L. Sorenson (Provo: Farms, 2000).

Carefully examining the geographical evidence in the account, it becomes clear that the Lamanite logistical system was dependent on keeping the pass at Antiparah open. The Lamanite supply route likely depended on canoes and boats ferrying supplies up the coast to a convenient landing point where they were stockpiled and then carried by land up through the pass to be distributed to the Lamanite occupational armies. The garrison at Antiparah guaranteed the safe passage of the supplies from the coast. Capturing Antiparah would cut the Lamanites in Manti off from their main source of supplies and seal the invasion route into the land of Zarahemla and the Sidon River valley.

Though there were land routes from the land of Nephi to the land of Manti, as demonstrated by the Battle of the Sidon River Crossing (though there were probably other routes as well), the advantages of bringing supplies on canoes via the ocean versus by porter overland were manifold. First, the most direct route to Manti—through the Sidon River Crossing—was probably heavily guarded by Nephite forces. Second, the overland routes were over terrain that was not conducive to the constant and rapid flow of logistical materials from Lamanite lands to the battlefront. In other words, these routes passed through heavily vegetated and hilly country that required a great deal of effort to cross and were probably disease-ridden, which was costly in terms of manpower that would more efficiently be employed as combat troops. However, on the other hand, the supplies coming up the coast were likely delivered in large canoes or by porters traveling on relatively flat terrain. The maritime route in particular allowed the Lamanites to ship more supplies faster and with fewer men than any supply column marching overland, a fact still true today. From their landing point, the overland trip to the Lamanite armies in the land of Manti was an easier task under the protection of the garrison at Antiparah.

Because of these considerations, any kind of Nephite threat to this logistics route would've been taken incredibly seriously. If a Nephite force were allowed to fortify the city on the western seashore, it could conduct forays against the supply columns that were coming up the coast, destroying them before they reached the pass, effectively cutting off Antiparah and Manti from their support system, their lifeline. The city on the western seashore was probably already fortified and lightly defended, but since the garrison was only sufficient to defend it, the Lamanites had until then just ignored it. However, Helaman's two thousand reinforcements who marched in that direction presented an entirely new scenario. This force would be strong enough to defend the city and launch raids against the Lamanite supply line. Thus the garrison of Antiparah felt compelled to destroy them before they reached the fortifications, behind which they could have held off a large army for some time. This may be why most of the garrison of Antiparah suddenly ventured out from their fortified position when they had steadfastly refused to do so until then. They had to crush those reinforcements with overwhelming force before they could become a significant threat. The Lamanites sent out most of their forces against Helaman, but prudently left a sufficiently strong force back in Antiparah to defend it.

Now, this analysis isn't something sure or certain. Mormon doesn't explain the reasons behind most of the Lamanite garrison leaving Antiparah in the text, likely because to a professional military man familiar with the terrain, the reasons were obvious and required no explanation. But with no map or local knowledge, it isn't so clear to readers living 1500-plus years later. Yet it's the inclusions of these seemingly sudden, illogical actions that speak volumes about the authenticity of the text and the military expertise of the author, as when all of the clues provided in the text are examined in depth, the logic becomes apparent. This is the sort of unconscious consistency in the war accounts that would be almost impossible for someone writing a made-up story—as Joseph Smith has been accused of—to get right. And yet the Book of Mormon gets them right repeatedly, with only a few exceptions that will be pointed out later.

So as soon as most of the Antiparah garrison was out in pursuit, Helaman's force turned, not back toward Judea, but north along the coast (Alma 56:36). When he was able to get between the Lamanite army and Antiparah, Antipus marched out after the Lamanites with part of his force. He left the rest of his force in Judea to prevent the Lamanites in Manti from attacking his rear and trapping his army between Antiparah and Manti (Alma 56:33).

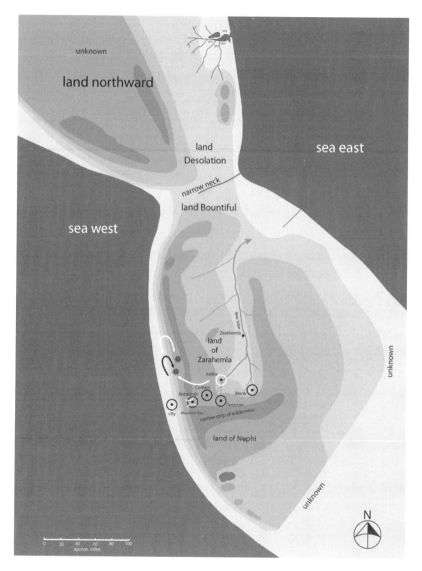

The Antiparah Maneuver, Move 3. Based on *Mormon's Map*. Courtesy of John L. Sorenson (Provo: Farms, 2000).

This was exactly what the Nephites hoped to accomplish, trapping the Antiparah garrison between Helaman's force and Antipus's force. Antipus's plan was for the Lamanites to turn and attack his army, giving Helaman the opportunity to turn and strike the Lamanites from the rear, catching them between two forces. However, the Lamanite army pursuing Helaman detected Antipus's army before the trap was fully in place. Perceiving the Nephite plan, the Lamanites pursued Helaman's force more vigorously, trying to overtake and destroy this small force first so they could deal with Antipus's army on more equal or advantageous footing (Alma 56:37). Antipus's army was already marching hard, but when he saw that the Lamanites weren't falling for the plan, Antipus forced his army to march even faster to prevent the Lamanites from destroying Helaman's men before his men were in place to support. Night came and all three forces camped for the night, exhausted from the day's tough marches (Alma 56:38).

The next morning, the Lamanites tried to get an early start, hoping to catch Helaman before his force could break camp. Helaman either anticipated this or was lucky; his force got away in time. To try and shake the Lamanites, Helaman took his forces slightly east, off of the coastal plain and into the wilderness. He was probably hoping that the rough terrain and vegetation would hide his men and slow down the larger pursuing force, but the Lamanite leaders drove their men and nipped the heels of the stripling warriors all day.

Meanwhile, Antipus's force seemed to take a little too much time to realize the Lamanites were on the move. Fearing the destruction of Helaman and his men, they began marching much harder than usual just to keep up. Antipus's concern about the stripling warriors was justified, as they were green and lacked combat experience. He was extremely fearful of what would happen should the Lamanites get to them before his forces could enter the battle. This fear was likely heightened by the fact that the Lamanites had a particular hate for the stripling warriors, who were ethnic Lamanites fighting on the side of the Nephites. They were considered to be traitors, and Antipus knew that the Lamanites would show absolutely no mercy should they catch them. Again, all three armies made camp for the night utterly exhausted (Alma 56:39–40), but that night the Lamanites developed their own counter-trap. Thus far, they hadn't worried about pursuing Helaman along the coast or through the wilderness because there were no Nephite forces in the area. However, after two days of forced marching, they were probably coming uncomfortably close to Ammonihah and Noah, where they knew there were strong Nephite garrisons that could carry out offensive operations.

The Lamanites were aware of Antipus's army, how far it had fallen behind, and just how desperately it was trying to prevent them from destroying Helaman's force—likely through spies. The Lamanites decided to change their objective, taking on the pursuing Nephites first by setting up an ambush for Antipus and his exhausted men to fall into. Thinking tactically, the Lamanite leaders believed this was the most effective way to punch a path through the Nephite ring and return to Antiparah.

The Lamanites expertly executed their counter-trap. As they did on the previous morning, they marched as early as possible toward Helaman's men, who proceeded to flee (Alma 56:41). Probably the entire Lamanite force made the initial drive on Helaman for visual effect, but then most turned back, with only a small force continuing to follow the stripling warrior's, making as much noise as possible to mimic the sounds of a large army (Alma 56:41–42). The Lamanites could also be adept at deception and psychological warfare. Helaman, an inexperienced leader with green troops, fell for the ruse, and his men fled as if being pursued by the entire Lamanite army.

Meanwhile, the remainder of the Lamanite army set up their trap, knowing that Antipus would follow the trail left by Helaman and the Lamanites and would take few precautions, not expecting the ambush. Antipus's objective was only to save Helaman and the stripling warriors from annihilation. To do so, he had to catch up. Caution would only slow him down, and he couldn't afford that. This lack of caution made him and his army easy targets. The Lamanites attacked the exhausted Nephites, likely specifically targeting the leaders. Without leadership, an army becomes disoriented and any cohesion rapidly breaks down. The record states that Antipus and many of the leaders were killed (Alma 56:51). The Nephite army began to fall apart and the Lamanites came near to victory. Had they been successful, there would have been little standing between the Lamanites in Manti and the city of Zarahemla. This struggle became critical as the Nephite trap basically backfired.

Meanwhile, Helaman and his stripling warriors finally noticed that they weren't being pursued and halted (Alma 56:42–43). Helaman, lacking experience, didn't know what to do next, and because of his precipitous rush, he had no information on his enemy's whereabouts;

whether the Lamanites had stopped because Antipus had caught up with them, whether the Lamanites had given up and turned back, or whether they were laying a trap for Antipus or the stripling warriors. Apparently his instincts (or divine guidance) told him to turn back to find the answers to these questions. If the Lamanites had set a trap, turning back could mean the destruction of his entire force, but he also knew that his force would be critical to Antipus if the Nephites had caught up with the Lamanites.

Knowing that any decision he made would be critical, he took the choice to his men, seeking their advice. This is another indication that Helaman and his men were volunteers rather than professional troops. Volunteers in armies are much more likely to share camaraderie with their officers than professionals who have been drilled in strict military discipline, hierarchy, and traditions. It proved to be a wise decision, and in the typical fashion of the guileless and patriotic youths that they were, the stripling warriors voted—down to the last man—to turn back, venture into the unknown, and triumph or die trying (Alma 56:42–47).

This decision proved to be one of the most important of the war, though Helaman and his men probably didn't know it at the time. Marching back toward where they had come, they could soon hear the sounds of battle and found the Lamanite armies in the process of routing the confused, leaderless Nephites. Helaman's band of stripling warriors—again demonstrating their amateurish and impulsive nature—immediately charged into the Lamanite rear with such fury that the entire army stopped and turned to face Helaman's onslaught (Alma 56:52). This detail speaks to the authenticity of the account because it's common for green troops with no real combat experience to show reckless courage in their first battle and frontally charge at the enemy positions. Veterans, while not by any means cowardly (but having seen the destructive effect of battle), tend to be much less prone to these types of impulsive acts.

But it was effective. This gave Antipus's army a much-needed boost in morale and sufficient time to reorganize and rally. Taking advantage of what had happened, the Nephites gathered courage, reformed their ranks, and attacked the Lamanites from what was now the rear as the stripling warriors' fierce onslaught hammered the Lamanites against the Nephite army anvil. After taking a heavy beating, the Lamanites dropped their weapons and surrendered (Alma 56:54).

The Nephite trap had worked, but only just—and at the cost of its planner, Captain Antipus, and many of his officers. This account rings authentic because it illustrates many well-known principles of war, like the difficulties of carrying out complicated maneuvers and the problems and advantages of inexperienced officers leading green armies. It also shows how an enemy doesn't always react as expected, even with the best plans. Finally, it demonstrates how plans can succeed despite Murphy's Law; apparently everything went wrong with their plan, but tactical offensive maneuvers (and no doubt some amount of divine guidance) saved the day. Had Helaman and his warriors delayed much longer or made the decision not to turn back, the battle would've been won by the Lamanites. The door to Zarahemla would've been left ajar, and without sufficient troops to defend it, the city would've likely fallen to its enemies. As a consequence, the war might have lasted longer, or the Nephites might have been forced to abandon the Sidon River valley to the Lamanites, moving their civilization north of the narrow neck of land long before they did in Mormon's lifetime about four hundred years later. For now, however, Zarahemla and the Sidon River valley were safe.

But the story didn't end there. Victory for the Nephites resulted in a new, unexpected problem. The Lamanites had surrendered quickly and the Nephites had taken more prisoners than they had anticipated. They had no place to keep them and thus were forced to assign a significant part of their army to march and guard them down to the land of Zarahemla. The remainder of the Nephite forces marched back to Judea where Helaman, now the ranking Nephite officer, took command of the entire Nephite force in the western theater (Alma 56:57). The Nephites, having failed to take the city of Antiparah, now began preparations for this task.

The Fall of Antiparah

Because of the defeat by Helaman and his stripling warriors, the Lamanites in the southwest were in a rather precarious position. The garrison at Antiparah had been greatly reduced. While still sufficiently strong to defend the city, there were insufficient troops to keep the mountain pass open for all their logistics traffic. And because of the disruption of the supply corridor from the coast, the garrison could now be starved into submission. To accomplish this, the Nephites laid siege to the city and made forays against the supply columns coming from Manti, on the landside. The garrison could do nothing but hopelessly watch, knowing that it was only a matter of time.

The Lamanite troops in Manti were probably much better off than their counterparts in Antiparah, as the land was sufficiently fertile to grow crops. Also, as previously mentioned, there were overland routes from the land of Nephi to supply goods, material, and manpower. But these endeavors occupied so many of their men that the armies couldn't conduct all three required functions: offense, defense, and logistics. They had to dedicate the bulk of their resources to defending the cities they had taken and providing for their own basic sustenance. To get offensive operations going again, they had to reopen their supply lines from the land of Nephi and release men from agricultural tasks, which therefore required reopening the pass at Antiparah and reestablishing the logistics route from the western sea.

Ammoron wrote Helaman a letter with a tempting and cunning proposal. He offered Helaman the city of Antiparah in exchange for the Lamanite prisoners he'd taken. Ammoron was laying a trap, knowing that Helaman's efforts to garrison Judea and Antiparah would stretch the Nephite manpower to its limit. Even if they could hold the cities with what they had, it would certainly reduce their mobility, an advantage Ammoron wanted. Furthermore, by offering Antiparah, Ammoron was offering nothing more than a city already on the brink of falling to Helaman's forces. Ammoron was basically offering to exchange nothing for something that would give the Lamanites great advantage in the region. While the Nephites forces would be stretched thin, the released Lamanite prisoners would add great strength to the Ammoron's armies in significant enough numbers to allow them to, in turn, lay siege to the Nephites at Antiparah and reopen the pass for seaborne provisions to Manti. With the renewed supplies, they could reinforce the Lamanites in Manti and then attempt forays against the weakened forces at Judea.

Helaman saw through this ploy and replied that he'd only agree to a prisoner exchange. Ammoron refused because this proposal gave neither side an additional advantage. The garrison at Antiparah was finally starved beyond resistance, and the Lamanites abandoned the city to Nephite hands. The door to Zarahemla in this quarter was thus shut to the Lamanites (Alma 57:1–5).

Chapter 7: Battle of the City of Mulek

Meanwhile, the Nephites faced an equally desperate situation in the northeast. In the twenty-fifth year, due to internal strife among the Nephites, the Lamanites took control of the previously mentioned eastern coastal cities, conquered Mulek, and marched to take the city of Bountiful (Alma 51:22–28). By taking Bountiful, they would cut off the Nephite escape routes to the north country, trapping them between two powerful Lamanite armies.

Captain Moroni sent his best local commander, Teancum, to the land of Bountiful to intercept and defeat Amalickiah's forces in a pitched battle at the border (Alma 51:29–32). When night fell, Teancum and his servant made a clandestine incursion into the Lamanite camp, where they assassinated Amalickiah as he slept, jabbing a javelin through his heart. The effort succeeded and Amalickiah died without making a sound, allowing Teancum to sneak back to his men and wake them up to prepare for battle. When the Lamanites found their leader dead and the Nephite armies ready for battle, they lost courage and retreated to their closest stronghold, the city of Mulek (Alma 51:37; 52:1–2).

In the twenty-sixth year, Amalickiah's brother, Ammoron, replaced him as king and commander of the Lamanite armies. He consolidated his hold on the conquered eastern cities and returned to the land of Nephi to open a second front by attacking along the western coast (Alma 52:12). He sought to take the pressure off of his armies in the east, giving them a greater chance of taking Bountiful and finally cutting off the

Nephites' escape route to the lands north. If the Nephites turned their attention to the east, the Lamanites would then be free to advance up the west coast. Either option meant a tough campaign for the Nephites to avoid the double envelopment strategy of the Lamanites.

However, the Nephites enjoyed one important advantage over the Lamanites. Though heavily outnumbered, the Nephites operated along interior lines, whereas the Lamanites operated along exterior lines,[13] which meant that the Nephites could shuttle forces back and forth more quickly than the Lamanites, and probably over more developed roads. However, even with this advantage, the Nephites were in a less-than-ideal situation. Their coordination, timing, and luck would have to be nearly perfect to overcome their enemies because of their smaller numbers.

To foil the Lamanite plan, Captain Moroni ordered Teancum to take back the city of Mulek, which would relieve pressure on the northeastern front (Alma 52:16). Mulek's importance to the Lamanites lay in it being a base from which they could mount attacks on the city of Bountiful. The city of Bountiful (as previously noted) was the gateway to the lands northward and the Nephite escape route should they be routed in the land of Zarahemla. Teancum noted the Lamanites' strength in the city of Mulek and informed Captain Moroni that his force was insufficient to take the city back (Alma 52:17). Teancum may have believed that the Nephites couldn't afford the level of casualties the Lamanites had suffered taking over the city previously. Moroni concurred and ordered him to concentrate instead on fortifying Bountiful and securing the northern pass. Moroni

---

13. To recap, *interior lines* are the lines within a defensive perimeter. By contrast, the attackers moving outside the defensive perimeter move on *exterior lines*. To get from one side of the perimeter to the other, attackers must move a far greater distance than defenders. This is one of the reasons that attacking always requires far greater numbers than defending because; when defending, it's relatively easy to move forces from one threatened point to another, whereas attacking requires a far greater effort to move the same number of forces. And to guarantee success, attackers usually have to apply at least twice if not three times as much force as defenders at the point of attack. See footnote 9 (page 54) for further information on interior and exterior lines.

also had Teancum, instead of letting Lamanite prisoners go after an oath (as done previously), keep prisoners that fell into his hands so they could be used as ransom for their own prisoners who had fallen into the Lamanite hands (Alma 52:8).

Captain Moroni said that he would make a personal visit to review the situation. After he stabilized security along the western seashore, Moroni marched with his army to Bountiful, where he, Teancum, and other officers held a meeting to develop new operational plans. They decided to attempt to draw the Lamanites out of the city, as had been done at Antiparah, seeking to overcome numerical inferiority with deception and maneuvers to gain the upper hand over the Lamanites (Alma 52:19).

They initially tried convention, sending an emissary to the enemy leader, proposing a time and a place for a battle. The Lamanite leader, a wary Zoramite whose name was Jacob, refused (Alma 52:20). There had already been too much unorthodox and "dirty" warfare to even consider more such from Captain Moroni. As it turned out, Jacob's fears were well founded.

After this initial failure, Captain Moroni did then resort to stratagem, adopting a battle plan similar to the previously described Antiparah operation. It's not clear exactly how much Moroni knew about the details of the Antiparah battle at this time, as he may have received Helaman's epistle at a later date, but he could've learned the details from a different source, given the striking similarities in the concept. However, Captain Moroni's battle plan was not a direct copy, but rather an interesting combination of Helaman's tactics at Antiparah and techniques Moroni had used successfully at the Battle of the Sidon River Crossing.

Captain Moroni sent a small force of men under Teancum along the shore on the east side of the city, hoping to tempt the Lamanites (Alma 52:22). They were undoubtedly told to be as noisy as possible so that the Lamanite scouts would be sure to discover them. They were probably also told to deliberately act unsuspecting so the Lamanites would believe that launching a rapid lightning attack would assure a quick victory.

In order to draw the entire Mulek garrison out to attack a small Nephite force, knowing they'd refused to meet outside the city earlier, would have required Moroni to dangle an irresistible prize in front of them. It's quite possible that was Teancum himself. Sending Teancum at the head of a small, weak force must have been more than Jacob the Zoramite could resist, as anyone who led the force that killed Teancum (the man who assassinated Amalickiah and stopped the Lamanite drive on Bountiful) was sure to receive great honor and promotion. Such a strike would also greatly decrease the morale of the Nephites, perhaps enough to finally crumble their will to continue defending the land of Bountiful. This is a likely explanation for why Jacob risked sending almost his entire force out on a reckless pursuit of the soldiers under Teancum northward into Bountiful, despite going perilously deep into Nephite territory.

However, Teancum's force was deliberately small for mobility and agility, all the while still appearing vulnerable. Teancum moved just close enough to the Lamanites to present a tantalizing prize, but far enough away to stay just out of their grasp. This would've increased the Lamanite's ardor, provoking them to throw caution to the wind and ignore the potential peril. The account indicates that in their mad chase after Teancum, the Lamanite army might have lost track of their location (in other words how far they were from Mulek and how deep they had penetrated into Nephite territory).

Meanwhile, Captain Moroni's army was concealed in the jungle to the west of the city, far enough away to avoid Lamanite scouts but close enough to quickly reach the city. As only a few Lamanites remained behind to guard the city, it was a relatively simple task to attack and overwhelm them (Alma 52:24–25). The account doesn't describe the assault, but by attacking at multiple locations, a small garrison would not have been able to man all the fortifications simultaneously, leaving inevitable gaps that would've been exploited by Moroni to penetrate the fortifications and surround the Lamanite defenders. There doesn't appear to have been much resistance, indicating that the garrison was successfully outflanked.

But Captain Moroni didn't content himself with merely taking the city. His second objective was to destroy the Lamanite army that was chasing after Teancum. Had he contented himself merely with taking Mulek, the returning Lamanite army could have conceivably threatened and retaken Mulek with superior force, not to mention the added advantage of having a perfect knowledge of the city's strengths and weaknesses. Alternatively, the army could bypass Mulek and just withdraw to the next fortified Lamanite city, at a minimum making the next fortification more difficult to take because of the additional forces—and likely serving as a point from which the Lamanites could launch attacks to recover Mulek as well. On Captain Moroni's side, garrisoning the city of Mulek meant his lines of communication would be lengthened and his forces spread thin while his enemies' own lines of communication would be shortened and their forces concentrated with the addition of Jacob's army. This might have been a situation in which their taking back Mulek actually weakened the Nephite position rather than strengthen it. For these reasons, the destruction of Jacob's army was vital to the Nephite war effort, perhaps more important than taking the city itself. Furthermore, destroying Jacob's army would deliver a tremendous blow to Lamanite morale, greatly weakening their resolve to fight future Nephite attacks.

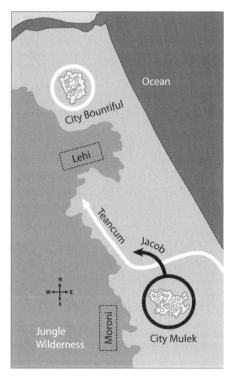

The Battle of the City of Mulek—phase 1.

Knowing this, Captain Moroni assumed the risk, leaving his own skeleton force in Mulek and immediately taking the bulk of his forces out of the city and into the most likely path that the Lamanites would take on their return from the wild goose chase (Alma 52:26). The risk was great, but given the overwhelming size of the Lamanite garrison returning to Mulek, it was also necessary if Moroni was to have any chance of destroying Jacob's army.

Teancum had led the Lamanites almost the entire way to the city of Bountiful and into a carefully laid trap. Teancum approached the Nephite army commanded by Lehi, who'd been assigned previously to garrison the city. They were awaiting the Lamanites arrival, probably arrayed in battle formation. Lehi's men began marching toward the Lamanites pursuing Teancum, though the account doesn't make it clear if Teancum's force joined Lehi or passed through and continued to march toward Bountiful (Alma 52:27).

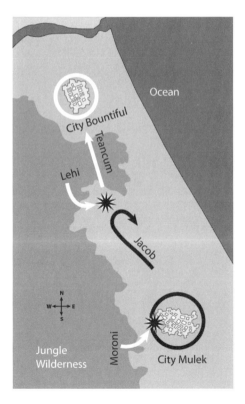

The Battle of the City of Mulek—phase 2.

The Lamanites at this point realized they'd fallen into a trap, made worse because Lehi's troops were fresh and the Lamanites were tired from the forced march. The realization of how far they'd gone from the city of Mulek sank in with horrifying suddenness, along with the recognition that their best hope was to make a mad dash back to Mulek (Alma 52:28). Their fear was being overtaken by Lehi's fresh troops and being forced to fight their way to sanctuary. The officers attempted to rally the strength of their men for a desperate dash, but in their haste failed to consider that a large Nephite force might already have taken up a position between them and the city.

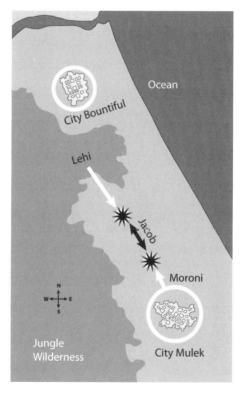

The Battle of the City of Mulek—phase 3.

Meanwhile, attempting to give Moroni time to reach the battle, Lehi sought to give the impression that he was giving heated chase to the Lamanites, though not so quickly that the battle would start before Captain Moroni's forces arrived from the south (Alma 52:30).

If the fighting began before that, Lehi's forces (which were not all that large) would've been in danger of being overwhelmed by the superior number of the Lamanites. Fortunately, Lehi had trained his troops well in the art of war. He and his men put on a convincing show, and the Lamanites—without stopping to consider their advantage—continued their headlong flight toward Mulek. Then suddenly they slammed into the forces of Captain Moroni. The Nephites probably thought that it would now be a relatively easy battle, but the Lamanite commander, Jacob, was determined to cut his way back through to Mulek with his numerically superior forces, no matter the cost. The Lamanites rallied from their initial shock and, ignoring their exhaustion, attacked with fury borne from desperation (Alma 52:33). Meanwhile, Lehi's attempt to moderate his pursuit had backfired to a degree because his army was still a ways behind Jacob's forces, so Captain Moroni's army took the full brunt of the Lamanites' assault.

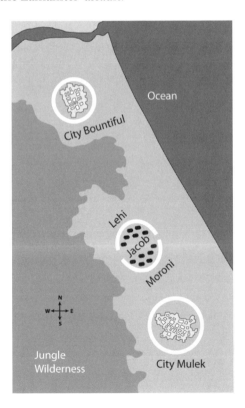

The Battle of the City of Mulek—phase 4.

The battle was so intense that Captain Moroni was wounded and Jacob was killed—in a scenario somewhat reminiscent of Helaman's stripling warriors' first battle (Alma 52:35). At this critical moment, Lehi's forces arrived and attacked the Lamanite rear echelons, catching them between two forces. Jacob's death produced a predictable result: confusion and panic, exacerbated by exhaustion, which caused unit cohesion to break down (Alma 52:36).

At this point, Captain Moroni stopped the killing, as he had during the battle at the Sidon River Crossing, again showing compassion to his enemies to avoid unnecessary bloodshed when possible. Moroni called out to the Lamanites to give up their weapons in exchange for their lives (Alma 52:37). The remaining leaders agreed, threw down their weapons, and commanded their men to do likewise. Those few who wouldn't were bound, and the huge mass of prisoners were marched to the land of Bountiful (Alma 52:38–39). Thus Captain Moroni both took the city of Mulek, rendered Jacob's army ineffective, recovered Nephite lands, reduced the threat to Bountiful, and even balanced the relative Nephite-Lamanite correlation of forces.

Prisoners of War

After the battle, Lehi assumed command of the city, replacing Teancum, who had been defending the city of Bountiful after arriving there once his mission was completed (Alma 53:2). Teancum was put in charge of the Lamanite prisoners, though his first task was to bury all of the dead and then march to Bountiful with the prisoners, where they were made to build ditch fortifications around the city (Alma 53:3).

The different tasks that were assigned to Lehi and Teancum reflects the differences in their personalities. Lehi was likely somewhat older than Teancum, more experienced, and more even-tempered. Teancum was courageous, bold to the point of recklessness, and aggressive, which made him just the man Moroni needed to extract maximum labor from their prisoners (but not as suited for administering and defending a city).

Such a task required a more experienced and steady personality, such as that of Lehi. The account also suggests that Lehi and Captain Moroni were perhaps more than just colleagues. They may have been close personal friends. When Captain Moroni visited Lehi in Mulek, they apparently had a heartfelt reunion, rejoicing in each other's safety (Alma 53:2).

Holding large numbers of prisoners is a drain on any army, as they must dedicate a sufficiently large force to ensure the prisoners remain captive and are fed and housed adequately. The Nephites' treatment of the Lamanite prisoners would be considered unlawful by today's standards, a violation of the Geneva Convention designed to reduce many of the morally repugnant practices of warfare. However, such conventions didn't exist in Book of Mormon times. First, Teancum forced his prisoners to bury the dead from both sides. After this, he marched them to the land of Bountiful where, under the orders of Captain Moroni, they built a new type of fortification, especially designed to hold the prisoners. They built a wall of tall tree trunks around the whole city, dug a ditch, and tossed dirt up against the outer wall of the timbers, forming a rather high wall. In essence, Moroni modified his defensive fortifications to keep people in rather than out, thus becoming an effective prison. The tall and vertical walls prevented prisoners from climbing them, and on the outside they were just as defensible as the other fortifications previously used (Alma 53:4–5).

Even though there was no Geneva Convention at that time, it's clear that Mormon felt a twinge of guilt about the Lamanite prisoners' forced labor. He goes out of his way to justify the action by noting that Captain Moroni didn't want to lose the initiative gained by capturing Mulek and he needed all his forces for further offensive operations. If his men had to take the time to construct the prisoner fortifications, the Lamanites might have then had sufficient time to reinforce and recover from their losses. Captain Moroni couldn't afford to give his enemies that advantage and decided to kill two birds with one stone (his shortage of manpower and the need for a prisoner-of-war camp to be constructed) by putting the prisoners to work. Furthermore, he found it easier to guard the prisoners while they were busy laboring than when they were idle (Alma 53:5). But as it was, he wasn't able to continue offensive operations for the remainder of that year. Instead, Moroni further strengthened his fortifications and used his troops to deliver aid to the homeless and hungry from the war (Alma 53:7).

Prisoner Exchange

As mentioned in Alma 52:8, prisoners of war could be taken to be used as ransom for prisoners held captive by the other side. In Alma 54, the exchange of letters between Moroni and Ammoron gives us a glimpse of how this worked. In previous battles, Lamanite prisoners had been forced to take an oath and were then released, much like the honor parole of European tradition during the eighteenth century. The prisoners taken in the Battle of Mulek were not forced to take an oath and were retained (indicating the sacredness of oath-taking, as a Lamanite soldier who had taken the oath wouldn't have much value for such exchanges).

Alma 54 shows why such exchanges were valuable. In this instance, Ammoron sent a letter to Captain Moroni, desiring that they exchange prisoners. Captain Moroni replied with a scalding condemnation of Ammoron and demands for an entire Nephite family (man, wife, and children) in exchange for each Lamanite soldier. Ammoron replied with an equally sarcastic letter, blatantly stating that he wanted to exchange prisoners, not for any humanitarian reasons but because he needed reinforcements to continue an eternal war. However, he was glad to give up a whole family for a single man because he wanted to preserve the food supply for his men and their coming battles (Alma 54:20). This letter from Ammoron convinced Captain Moroni to seek another way to liberate the Nephite prisoners.

Chapter 8: The Cities of Cumeni and Manti

In the western theater, the war began to move again. Helaman received 6,060 reinforcements, which he decided he'd use to lay siege to the city of Cumeni (Alma 57:6). This was a traditional siege, though without ancient eastern or medieval siege engines. Helaman's force was too weak to assault the city directly, so he instead attempted to starve the defenders into submission. He may have blocked access to the city by building up a wall of fortifications similar to the ones defending the city. Though the text isn't explicit, some important clues support this idea.

The outer ring actually served to trap the Lamanite defenders inside, allowing Helaman's smaller forces to surround and contain a larger force. Also, based on the following evidence, it is likely that Helaman's fortifications didn't form a continuous ring around the entire city, but instead relied on building fortifications on critical terrain to control all of the ingress and egress routes. The Lamanites were forced to try and break the siege by attacking Helaman's outer ring at night to avoid heavy casualties from assaulting fortified positions. Also, attacking at night offered a better chance of penetrating the gaps between the Nephite fortifications. However, all such attempts failed with heavy casualties (Alma 57:9). Fortifications had previously been used to keep forces from assaulting cities; now they were being used to contain a defending force inside a city. Despite the failure, the Lamanites in the city still far outnumbered the besieging Nephite army and refused to give up for many days.

In desperation, the Lamanite supply column prepared for one last attempt to penetrate the Nephite noose from the outside and deliver provisions to the besieged troops. The strongest evidence for an external ring of fortifications comes from the passages describing this event. The account states that when the Lamanites tried to take the provisions into the city at night, they thought they had entered the city, but in reality they had walked right into the heart of the Nephite positions surrounding the city, so the provisions and carriers were captured by the Nephites (Alma 57:10). This could only have happened if the Nephite positions looked similar enough to the defenses around the city that the Lamanite supply column would've confused them with their own. Before the city surrendered, the prisoners and provisions from the supply column were sent down to the land of Zarahemla. Shorty after this, and possibly as a result, the Lamanite garrison lost all hope of receiving reinforcements, supplies, or breaking out of the city and they surrendered to Helaman (Alma 57:12).

Prisoners in the West

The fall of the city of Cumeni yielded such an immense number of prisoners that all of the besieging force were pressed into guard duty. The difficulties of attending to such a large number of prisoners caused many of the Lamanites to become disgruntled with their lot and, realizing they far outnumbered their captors, sought to rush the few guards present, overpower them, and escape. The small number of guards vis-à-vis the prisoners meant that only a small percentage would be killed before the majority either escaped or took control.

This tense situation was probably exacerbated by the fact that the Nephites didn't have enough provisions to feed both themselves and the Lamanite prisoners, despite having captured Lamanite supplies (Alma 57:14–15). Perhaps it was hunger that provoked the Lamanite prisoner to rebel. They had been reluctant to surrender in the first place and had only done so to avoid starvation. However, the food situation likely hadn't improved in captivity, and even threatened to worsen, so the Lamanites faced death soon anyway. Better they retain some honor, take their chances, and rush the guards. Under these sort of circumstances, dodging a guard's sword gave a man more of a chance than remaining a prisoner.

Helaman was now more decisive. The prisoner revolt forced him to impose order by killing a large numbers of them, after which he sent the remainder down to Zarahemla, escorted by half his troops. The rest of his forces maintained the city of Cumeni (Alma 57:16).

Just as part of the army was taking the prisoners to Zarahemla, a Lamanite army, with its logistical train, struck Cumeni. The Nephites in Cumeni found themselves in danger of being overrun. However, luck saved the city. As the Lamanite army began their attack, some Nephite scouts ran into the Nephite column who were guarding the prisoners. Perhaps they'd been sent to call the men back, perhaps it was just a chance encounter, but—out of breath and agitated—the scouts yelled out that there was a Lamanite army attacking Cumeni. When the prisoners heard this, they broke out in large numbers and attacked the guards. Many of the prisoners were slain and the rest fled. The Nephites realized that they couldn't catch the prisoners and it was more important that they save the city, so they rushed back just in time to reinforce the garrison.

Their arrival was sufficient to repel the Lamanite attack and inflict heavy casualties on the assaulting troops. The Lamanites fell back to the city of Manti (Alma 57:17–18, 22, 30–35).

The Battle of the City of Manti

The final Nephite objective in the western theater was to take back the city of Manti. However, taking this city was much more difficult than the other operations because the Lamanites had built up their strength faster than the Nephite forces. It's possible the Lamanites had been preparing for another offensive against the Nephites, attempting to retake some of the lost land and cities. The Nephite supply lines were much more precarious than those of the Lamanites, in part due to the internal turmoil in the land of Zarahemla, unbeknownst to Helaman. His men came close to starving to death, but finally food arrived with two thousand reinforcements (Alma 58:7).

Meanwhile, both the Lamanites and the Nephites made forays, seeking to draw each other into battle (Alma 58:6). The Nephites hoped again to draw the Lamanites out of their strongholds by teasing them with small forces. Having been fooled one too many times, the Lamanites didn't take the bait, or at least they desisted pursuing the

Nephite forces once these passed into terrain disadvantageous to the Lamanites (Alma 58:1). The Lamanites made similar efforts to entice the Nephites into battle that similarly failed.

Helaman's epistle to Moroni speaks of forays and difficulty with offensive operations because of numerous Lamanite strongholds and retreats (Alma 58:6). This may indicate that the Lamanites had developed a type of fortified defense—a network of fortified places north of Manti. This type of system would've allowed the Lamanites to hold a relatively long line with an economy of force because they wouldn't have had to garrison all of the line with equal strength everywhere. The strongholds of the line would have been built atop dominant terrain in checkerboard patterns in such a way so as to offer mutual support to neighboring strongholds, using the space between the fortified positions as kill zones to draw in and trap unsuspecting Nephite forces. The holds would've also served as concentration and jumping-off points from which to launch fierce local forays or counterattacks. A possible scenario would've been for the Lamanites to launch a foray and then retreat in such a way that they would draw an unsuspecting Nephite force into one of the kill zones, trap it in the midst of these strongholds, and retreat. One or more of the forts would then serve as an anvil while the forces in other forts would sally forth and hammer the Nephite force against the anvil. How successful the Lamanites were isn't clear, but the fact that Helaman mentions they were making little progress against the Lamanites probably means that some Nephite forces had fallen into such traps. This is one of the few times in the entire Book of Mormon that Lamanite ingenuity and adaptability are mentioned, but the reference is made casually in passing and is frustratingly brief.

Helaman put his mind to the task of dealing with the Lamanites in the city of Manti, seeking a way to bypass the Lamanites defense system. After receiving fresh reinforcements and food, Helaman began developing a plan for tricking the Lamanites into leaving the city, drawing on the combination of lessons and successful tactics he had employed in the Antiparah maneuver and those Captain Moroni had employed at the battle of the Sidon River Crossing. He took a force of men and his two trusted captains, Gid and Teomnor, and marched his forces south, far around the Lamanites, through the wilderness and deep into the enemy rear instead of attempting to break through the

Lamanite deathtrap network of retreats and fortifications in the north. The Lamanites made the mistake of thinking the Nephites couldn't march their armies through the heavily vegetated and mountainous route and thus failed to guard it. Helaman's force then set up camp in the wilderness to the south of the city of Manti and waited to be discovered by Lamanite scouts (Alma 58:13–14).

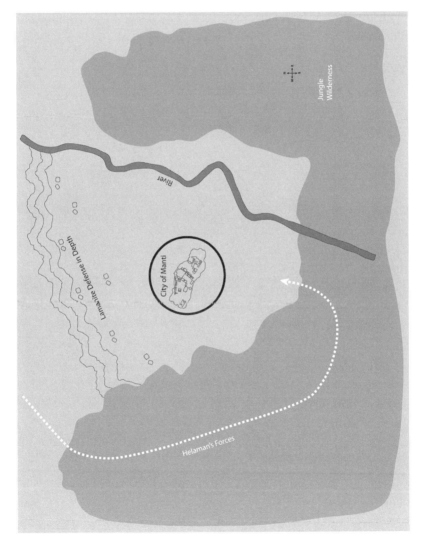

The Battle of the City of Manti—phase 1.

This wasn't long in coming. The threat that Helaman's forces posed to Manti was obvious, as they positioned in such a way that they could cut off the last land supply route from Lamanite lands into Manti (Alma 58:15). As it happened back with the Antiparah maneuver, the Lamanites were forced to react because Helaman threatened to cut their logistical line. When scouts were sent out from Manti to determine the overall strength of the Nephite forces, they discovered that they were not many in number, so the Lamanite forces began making preparations to attack them.

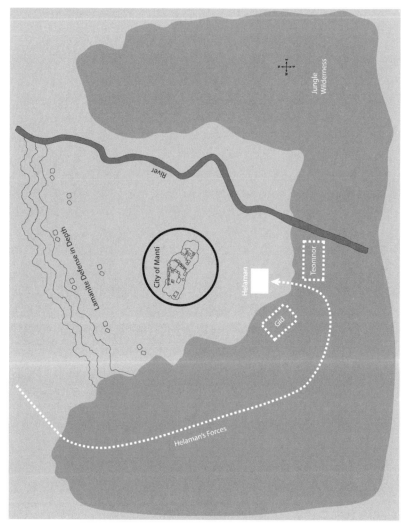

The Battle of the City of Manti—phase 2.

Helaman's own scouts reported the Lamanite activity, and he began to make demonstrations carefully designed to give the impression that his force didn't suspect the actions of the Lamanites. Along the main approach to his camp, he dispatched two small forces, one under Gid and the other under Teomnor, and ordered them to take up hidden positions to the left and right of the main path (Alma 58:16–17).

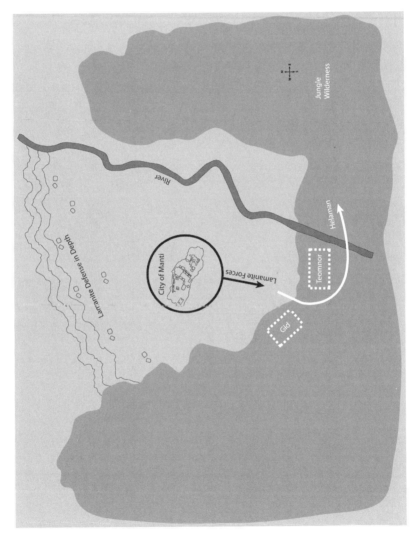

The Battle of the City of Manti—phase 3.

Meanwhile, Helaman kept up the appearance that everything was business as usual in the Nephite camp, seeking to allay any Lamanite suspicions so they would approach without much caution. Helaman's maturity as a commander since the Antiparah maneuver is evident in this account, as his forces coolly waited until the last moment before fleeing from the Lamanite forces dispatched to destroy them. This was an essential component of the plan because, by keeping up these appearances, Gid and Teomnor remained completely undetected.

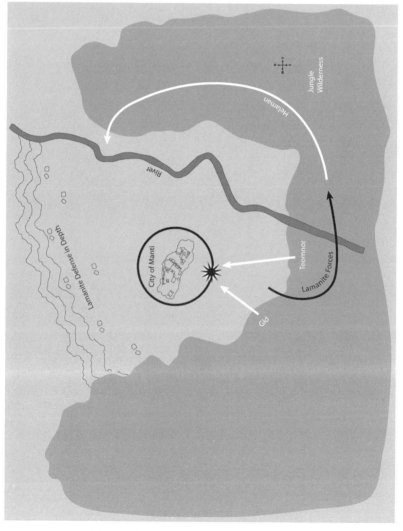

The Battle of the City of Manti—phase 4.

As the Lamanite forces approached Helaman's camp, he fled south toward Lamanite lands and began making a slow circuit through the wilderness, heading northward toward the land of Zarahemla. In the deep jungle, it's easy to lose one's bearing. Helaman was probably counting on this to fool the pursuing Lamanite force. Perhaps he was heading for the Sidon River Crossing, where Zarahemnah's army had been defeated.

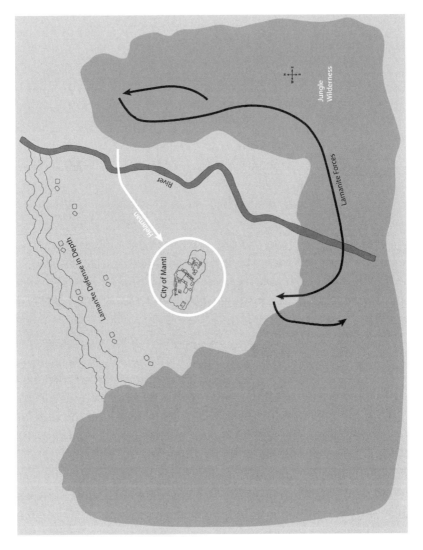

The Battle of the City of Manti—phase 5.

While this was going on, Gid and Teomnor led their forces and attacked the guards left in the city of Manti. The account says that they made short work of these guards, so evidently only a few soldiers had been left behind (Alma 58:20–21). Once again, the Lamanites were careless, though this is puzzling in the light of previous experiences. Perhaps the Lamanites were not all that good about sharing lessons learned from their defeats, but more probable is the fact that Jacob's army from Mulek had been almost entirely killed or captured. This meant there would've been little chance of writing lessons-learned reports about the Nephites' tactics used to defeat them, much less having the chance to disseminate them. At any rate, it's obvious that the guards left in Manti completely unsuspected Gid and Teomnor's maneuver, nor did they fear a Nephite force from the north because of the interlocking network of fortified positions and retreats between Manti and the Nephite positions in Cumeni.

Teomnor and Gid soon took the city. Meanwhile, Helaman must have been taking an extremely long and circuitous route to Zarahemla. It wasn't until late in the day that the Lamanite army realized they were chasing him and his forces toward Zarahemla. Again, to march an army deep into enemy territory like this on a disciplined circuitous route shows the maturity of both Helaman's leadership and his men. It isn't natural to march away from safety for long, or to march in such a fashion to deceive a large army and prevent it from realizing it was marching into harm's way for the better part of a day.

Once the Lamanites realized they were heading straight toward Zarahemla and not Nephi, they stopped pursuing and began retracing their steps (Alma 58:23–24). However, because it was late, darkness soon fell and the Lamanites, weary from the chase, camped for the night. In another show of discipline, Helaman forced his tired troops to continue marching all through the night, probably crossing the Sidon River and back toward Manti (Alma 58:26). They didn't reach the city that night, but when morning came they were much closer to Manti than the Lamanite army. They succeeded in joining Gid and Teomnor in Manti long before the enemy army arrived. When the Lamanites finally reached the city, they were dumbfounded that the Nephites had captured it (Alma 58:29). Apparently this possibility had never occurred to the Lamanite commanders, and their astonishment led to inaction. Rather than attack, they fled toward the land of Nephi. Had they attacked, they might have overcome Helaman's forces, as most of them had been marching for more than twenty-four hours and were exhausted. The Lamanites, meanwhile, were relatively fresh after their overnight camp. However, this is one of those cases common in war where the unexpected causes inertia, inaction, and ultimately defeat.

Possession of the city of Manti did two things for the Nephites. First, it sandwiched the Lamanite network of retreats and strongholds between two Nephite armies, rendering this network useless because its entire purpose had been to prevent the Nephites from making a drive on Manti from the north. Second, the Lamanite forces were now cut off from their supply route. It's no wonder Helaman states that after the fall of the city, all the Lamanite forces in that part of the land began to leave. Without their pivot, Manti, the whole Lamanite defensive structure and concentration point for renewed offensive was untenable (Alma 58:30). The only problem Helaman faced was that his forces were overextended. But because Helaman had done the unexpected, the Lamanites—instead of taking the offensive and attacking Helaman's exposed positions—gave up and fled.

Helaman

The story of the campaign in the west reveals a significant amount of information about the military capabilities of Helaman and his men. When they'd first arrived in the western theater, both leader and troops were inexperienced and unknowledgeable in the art and science of war. Their "greenness" was evident during the Antiparah maneuver, as the stripling warriors were easily provoked into rash action and Helaman hesitated in his decision-making when he was faced with the possible death of his men. Military commanders know they must develop a thick skin for their command to be effective because they must make tough life-and-death decisions that seem cruel and callous to civilians, but in the long run prevent greater bloodshed and win battles. They have to knowingly order men to their deaths to preserve the greater whole. Helaman didn't possess these qualities at first, as his precipitous and timid actions in the Antiparah maneuver revealed. He had obviously been chosen to lead the troops for his spiritual abilities rather than his military prowess at the time.

One of the messages the Book of Mormon teaches is that Helaman's spiritual strength influenced his decision-making in life as well as in his military responsibilities. This was apparently the case as he and his men made the right choices and the Nephites were then able to win crucial battles. However, in the Antiparah maneuver, Helaman's forces didn't arrive in time to save Antipus, the overall Nephite commander, and thus Helaman found himself thrust into command despite his lack of experience. However, Helaman rose to the challenge because his reliance on divine guidance made up for his lack of formal military training.

The idea of trapping the forces in Cumeni within the walls of the city by utilizing the same type of fortifications to keep people out of the city was brilliant. Perhaps it wasn't an original idea, but often the genius of military commanders isn't in their originality, but rather in their recognition, combination, and implementation of ideas developed by others. This was the case with both Moroni and Helaman. Taking Manti by stratagem was an operation as brilliant as anything that had been accomplished by Captain Moroni. Gid and Teomnor were Helaman's most trusted subordinates precisely because they were the type of officers who were full of ideas that Helaman could draw on. Helaman borrowed from his own experience as well as the collective Nephite experiences. At the battle of Manti, he overcame some difficult problems: how to bypass strong fortifications, how to draw a strong enemy out of its sanctuary, and when to take great risks (even though they were calculated). Had anything in his plan gone wrong, his small forces would've been slaughtered, but he acted coolly and professionally, waiting until the last minute to more easily draw their enemies into the trap. He marched deep into enemy territory, then lured the Lamanites toward Nephite lands and after all that still had the discipline to march all night and reach the objective before the Lamanites could react. His gamble paid off handsomely.

These things take charisma, nerve, decision-making capabilities, command presence, and genius. Helaman apparently possessed some of these skills naturally before becoming a commander and acquired the rest during his tenure as a leader. It must be said that by the time he carried out the maneuver to take the city of Manti, his forces were experienced and disciplined enough to carry it out, which brings up a further point—a good commander is in touch with his men. He knows what they can and can't do, and Helaman used this knowledge to gain advantage over his enemies.

Though Helaman is more known in the Book of Mormon for his spiritual qualities and leadership, it's evident that he was every bit as brilliant a military commander as Captain Moroni. He was the leader of the lesser theater of the war, though important all the same because of its proximity to Zarahemla. The terrain was probably not nearly as favorable to fight on; he received less support, received fewer forces and resources, and—in the author's view—was a less-heralded hero of the war accounts. Nevertheless, he was deserving of more praise, for he accomplished nearly as much as other Nephite war heroes.

Chapter 9: Gid and Dissent in Zarahemla

W e now return to the eastern theater of war. When last we left this theater, Captain Moroni and Ammoron had exchanged epistles regarding prisoner exchange. Ammoron's sarcasm and boldness in his reply epistle angered Captain Moroni (Alma 55:1), though Mormon seems to completely fail to consider how Captain Moroni's epistle was provocative to Ammoron, even if what he'd written in it was true. As a consequence, Captain Moroni decided that there was little point in exchanging prisoners; instead, he chose to retain the Lamanite prisoners while secretly conducting a military operation to liberate the captive Nephites. His intention was to strengthen his own army and deny the same advantage to the Lamanites (Alma 55:2–3).

Captain Moroni found out, probably through his scouts, that the Lamanites held their prisoners in the conquered city of Gid, not too far from Mulek. Despite losing Mulek to Moroni, the Lamanites hadn't bothered to move their prisoners, which might be an indication that the Lamanites had grown weary of the war and were becoming sloppy (perhaps due to the loss of senior leaders who hadn't been replaced). This war weariness was manifest in an overall lack of discipline, even among the officers, as the following events showed. Moroni sought to take advantage of the situation.

Trickery and deception were again employed in order to free the prisoners. Moroni searched the ranks of his army to see if there were any Lamanite deserters among his troops to lead the mission. He found the servant of the original Lamanite king who'd been assassinated by Amalickiah (Alma 55:4–5). With an obvious grudge against Amalickiah and his brother, Ammoron, the servant agreed to carry out the mission. He and some other men—possibly other Lamanite deserters—went to Gid with a large cargo of strong wine that had been especially prepared for the mission. They claimed to have escaped from the Nephites and in the process stolen a large provision of wine. The bored Lamanite garrison troops apparently bought the story and could hardly contain themselves as they were probably not a high priority on the resupply list. On top of that, they probably hadn't seen good wine for quite some time.

According to the account, the "escapees" managed to provoke the soldiers further by suggesting that they keep the wine until just prior to going to battle (Alma 55:8–10). This may indicate a common practice among certain armies—that of getting intoxicated prior to fighting—sometimes using alcohol, narcotics, or some other chemical to enhance senses, reduce inhibitions, or endow the soldiers with a feeling of invulnerability. In reality, this practice dulls the senses and makes soldiers less sensitive to pain and fear, thus endowing the user with an enhanced sense of valor. Unfortunately, it can also impact the ability of a soldier to think properly, making them more—not less—vulnerable.

At any rate, when the deserter Lamanites suggested waiting until just before battle to a bored garrison that hadn't been in a battle—and didn't have a prospect of going into battle for some time, it seems—the suggestion made the Lamanite soldiers even more determined to consume the alcohol immediately. They argued that if they did go into battle, they would probably be issued some additional wine, but in the meantime why let the good wine before them go to waste? The escapees *relented*, telling the Lamanites that they could do whatever they wanted (Alma 55:11–12).

The Lamanite garrison at Gid started drinking freely, becoming rather drunk within a few hours. Once the soldiers were all drunk, the escapees left and reported to Captain Moroni (Alma 55:13–15). Though there's no mention in the text, Captain Moroni must have secretly moved his army to a secluded location near the city, where he met up with his Lamanite agents and sent them back into the city with men loaded down with extra weapons. Silently, they climbed the outer defenses, and without ever entering the city, distributed the extra weapons to all of the prisoners: men, women, and even children, if they could carry one.

Meanwhile, the rest of the army surrounded the city and waited until morning (Alma 55:16–22). When the Lamanites woke up hung over from the previous night's drinking, they discovered they were surrounded both on the inside and outside the city walls by armed Nephites. Recognizing that their situation was hopeless—and likely not being in any condition to retaliate—they surrendered themselves (Alma 55:23–24). Thus by stealth and deception the Nephites captured another important city and its garrison and liberated a large number of Nephite prisoners.

The account of this operation may be true, but it is problematic because there are several incongruences in the account. It's hard to believe that a small party of Lamanite deserters could carry enough wine to intoxicate an entire garrison, considering the geographical setting is the American continent and there's no mention of beasts of burden being employed. The account never says just how large the Lamanite garrison was, but after it surrendered, it was large enough that the prisoners were able to build further fortifications around the city under Captain Moroni's direction (Alma 55:25). It's possible the city was quite small; however, this seems a bit unlikely, as the freed prisoners from Gid "greatly strengthened" Captain Moroni's armies (Alma 55:24).

The armies on both sides numbered from the thousands to tens of thousands, so it can be assumed that a substantial assistance meant at least a thousand able-bodied men or more among the prisoners in that camp—and the likelihood is that there were many more, as Helaman admits that his two thousand stripling warriors were a little army (Alma 56:33). It's perhaps reasonable to assume that a substantial number to the Nephites was somewhere above five thousand, though men weren't the only prisoners held at Gid. There were probably at least three women and children for every man there, so this would make the likely minimum total number of prisoners somewhere in the vicinity of 20,000 and possibly many more. The size of garrison required to guard such a large group and simultaneously defend the city from assault was probably in the vicinity of one to two thousand men, or in other words about one Lamanite soldier for every ten to twenty prisoners.

Returning to the original issue, whether there were a thousand or two thousand in the garrison, it's difficult to believe that a small group of men, even if they had beasts of burden, could carry enough alcohol to get even a thousand men entirely drunk. What's more likely is that the escapees were able to get the Lamanite sentries (perhaps between thirty and a hundred) at a sector of the fortifications drunk. This is a more plausible scenario, as the account doesn't state that the Nephites entered the city, but rather it says they surrounded it. If the entire garrison had been drunk, the Nephites could have marched in at will. Instead, they got on top of the walls or fortifications and, without making noise, "cast" weapons in for the Nephite prisoners (Alma 55:16). That they needed to use stealth for this task indicates they feared discovery, believing that this would lead to a bitter fight, or even completely jeopardize the operation.

Such a stealthy entry would logically have occurred in the single sector where the guards were drunk. It was essential to arm the prisoners so they would be able to take on the garrison while the Nephites on the outside assaulted the fortifications. The attack wasn't launched during the night, likely to prevent a bloody and confused melee with many casualties, and perhaps fratricide (fighting between friendly forces). In the dark of night, the Lamanites might have thought a few prisoners had overpowered their guards, stolen the weapons, and were attempting to escape, so Captain Moroni wanted to wait until daylight so the Lamanite garrison could fully appreciate their predicament. He gambled that upon seeing what they were up against—overwhelming force on the inside and a strong Nephite army ready for an assault on the outside—the Lamanite leaders would then realize the futility of resistance and choose to capitulate. Captain Moroni judged correctly, and the city fell into his hands without spilling a single drop of blood on either side.

Between the original written account and his abridgement and retelling of the story, Mormon quite possibly left out some crucial facts. This may have been a problem in the original text, or it may have been clear in Mormon's mind, but his retelling didn't make it clear to the reader. Perhaps this is the kind of thing that Mormon asks the reader to overlook when he speaks of the imperfections in his writing and use of language (Ether 12:25; Mormon 9:31).

By retaking the city of Gid, Captain Moroni scored yet another brilliant victory, regaining another fortified city, capturing an entire Lamanite garrison intact and without bloodshed—thus weakening the enemy forces—and replenishing his own forces without a prisoner exchange. It's interesting that after Captain Moroni liberated the Nephite prisoners, his forces no longer retained prisoners, having little use for them because the two sides no longer contemplated prisoner exchanges. In subsequent battles, Captain Moroni returned to the old method of obliging the captured to take an oath that they wouldn't return to fight against the Nephites and releasing them (Alma 62:15–16, 27–28).

To the Lamanites, these prisoners signified a great loss of manpower and a tempting target. They attempted several ruses of their own to free the captured Lamanites (Alma 55:27). While the account doesn't go into great detail, it says that on several occasions the Lamanites tried to encircle the Nephites at night, though they lost many prisoners this way (Alma 55:29). Night combat and maneuvering is a tricky business, even today with our advanced night vision technology, so it would've been much more so during Moroni's time. Apparently the Lamanites were *not* expert in this type of maneuver. The account doesn't say much about the method used by the Nephites to acquire more prisoners, but it's a lot easier to make short thrusts from a fixed position in a single direction at night than it is to try and carry out a complicated encircling maneuver.

The account says the Lamanites also attempted to poison or drug Nephite wine, no doubt having learned from the Nephites. However, the Nephites proved immune to such ploys and began testing all of the wine on Lamanite prisoners, drinking only what proved to be safe, meaning what didn't kill or make the prisoners ill (Alma 55:30–32). While such practices would be considered cruel, unusual, and utterly unlawful treatment of prisoners today, it was considered a completely legitimate practice then, as Mormon mentions it casually and makes no apology for the Nephites actions. In fact, he mentions it as an example of Nephite ingenuity, an inspiration and success granted them through their faithfulness to and trust in God. As a result, the Nephites managed to successfully avoid all intrigue and scheming on the part of the Lamanites, and the large numbers of Lamanite prisoners remained in their hands.

Zarahemla Dissent

Toward the end of the twenty-ninth year of the reign of the judges, Moroni prepared to take the Lamanite stronghold of Morianton. These preparations continued for over a year. In the meantime, he received a letter from Helaman, who sent a detailed account of the war effort in the western theater, offering the good news that things were going well. However, Helaman also noted that he hadn't received reinforcements or supplies as he should have. Captain Moroni responded by sending a letter to the chief judge, Pahoran, asking him to send Helaman men and provisions (Alma 59:1–3).

At this time, the Lamanite king, Ammoron, marched up at the head of a large army and supply column from the land of Nephi to Morianton. When ready, Ammoron's army launched an assault against the city of Nephihah, which, much to Captain Moroni's disgust, capitulated. Moroni's anger was no doubt based on his experience that it was less costly to defend a city than to attack it, and he had lost one more city that should have held out against Ammoron's siege. His anger increased when he learned that a major contributing factor to its surrender was that forces from Zarahemla had never arrived to reinforce the besieged garrison. At this point, he began doubting the resolve of the people, especially that of the Nephite government. The failure to send reinforcements led Captain Moroni to the conclude that the government and people weren't exerting their full effort, in essence holding back while his men and armies sacrificed their lives to keep the government in power and the people safe from the Lamanite threat (Alma 59:5–13).

Unable to understand or accept such inaction, Captain Moroni wrote a stinging letter to Pahoran, reminding him of his appointed duty to raise and equip armies and to requisition provisions to supply them properly. Moroni reminded Pahoran that his failure had resulted in his men fighting and dying in hunger because of their government's neglect. Captain Moroni then attacked politicians in general and made a blunt comparison between the current government and Amalickiah and the king men.

Moroni's sentiments aren't atypical among military leaders, who often show contempt for politicians, whom they see as full of talk but short on action and willing to send others to do their dangerous or dirty work. Captain Moroni nearly worked himself into an apoplectic fit at this point, driving home the point that, to him, the root cause of the war was power-seekers in government, politicians, and those aspiring to become king. He taunted Pahoran, asking if he hadn't become a traitor just like the king men. He ended his epistle with the ultimatum that either Pahoran comply with his duty to raise armies and send provisions or Captain Moroni would launch a revolution and overthrow the government. He rationalized that he wouldn't let the suffering and death of his men be in vain (Alma 60:1–36). Writing such a letter today would terminate the career of any commanding officer, or at least begin an interminable feud between that commander and the head of government.

Moroni's epistle was a potential disaster, but Pahoran swallowed his pride and wrote a much more understanding and conciliatory answer. He started out by forgiving Captain Moroni for his anger and threatening tone, unequivocally stating that he wasn't merely interested in power, and proceeded to explain the rational behind his actions, including why the Nephite armies had been neglected by the government. In the end, however, Captain Moroni had been right about the general nature of the problem, as the king men had indeed reemerged, convincing many of the people of Zarahemla to drive Pahoran and his government out of the city and into a sort of exile in the land of Gideon (Alma 61:1–21).

The population's war weariness was a likely factor in the king men's success, bringing to mind more recent historical examples such as the New York City draft riots during the American Civil War or the Paris Commune. War weariness has often led to internal revolution, as may have been the case of the revolution in Zarahemla.

The mixed ethnic nature of Nephite society could've also been a contributing factor. Why should the Mulekites, Zoramites, and Jaredite remnants continue to sacrifice and fight for a government dominated by the Nephites? Better yet, why not end the fighting and recover the throne? It's also possible that the Lamanites were involved, secretly communicating with specific king men, running what today is known as information warfare, meaning a covert operation to subvert their enemies and their will to fight.

An observation worth noting is that the rebellion had overcome Zarahemla, but it didn't spread to other lands or cities, indicating that it may have been confined to a particular ethnic group, most likely the Mulekites, who were concentrated in the land of Zarahemla and thus had more recent historical claims to the crown. Meanwhile, Pahoran had gathered an army in Gideon, one large enough that the king men dared not attack, but also not large enough for Pahoran to attack and defeat the king men.

As the rebellion hadn't spread any further than the capital city, the king men made contact with the Lamanites and offered to make an alliance with them. They promised to hold the city of Zarahemla, therefore preventing men and supplies from reaching the front until the Lamanite armies could arrive (Alma 61:8). This was the plan followed by Ammoron when he came down from the land of Nephi with a large army to continue the war. First, by leading the attack personally, he would make sure it was done right. Second, because of the secret deal with the king men, he felt confident of success and would march at the head of the army that would enter triumphantly into Zarahemla.

Renewed Lamanite Campaign

The capture of the city of Nephihah was the beginning of a new Lamanite campaign to drive toward the city of Zarahemla. Between the king men army in Zarahemla and a Lamanite army on the west coast, Helaman's army was held in check. Part of the Lamanite army would try to bottle up Captain Moroni and his troops in a pocket around the city of Bountiful. The more this Lamanite army could block men and supplies and keep them from reaching Moroni's army, the more likely it would then succeed in the rest of its conquest. The remainder of the Lamanite armies under the direction of Ammoron himself were to drive down the Sidon River valley and smash the hastily assembled, untrained Nephite army under the inexperienced leadership of Pahoran.

To stop this new Lamanite campaign—and perhaps recognizing his lack of experience leading an army—Pahoran implored Captain Moroni to leave the northeast armies in the care of Lehi and Teancum (to whom he had sent some provisions), take charge of the Nephite army at Gideon, and speedily move against the dissenters who were holding Zarahemla. In this, Pahoran hoped to foil the Lamanite plan (Alma 61:15).

Captain Moroni was satisfied that Pahoran wasn't a traitor after all and promptly complied, demonstrating his recognition that Pahoran was in charge. The only question remaining relates to why Pahoran failed to communicate his situation to Moroni earlier. History has always shown the importance of keeping military commanders informed of all security issues related to politics and, more important, of all political issues related to security, especially if the country is at war and an internal rebellion is even hinting of brewing. Perhaps Pahoran was embarrassed and hoped to solve the problem without distracting Moroni. Or maybe the retreat from Zarahemla to Gideon and its attendant administrative issues prevented Pahoran from writing to Moroni. Or it could be that in the haste to leave Zarahemla Pahoran had lost track of Captain Moroni's whereabouts and Moroni's letter reestablished the link. It's hard to imagine that appealing for help from his army commander wouldn't have been one of the first things Pahoran would've thought about; however, the question should be asked: If Moroni's courier was able to find Pahoran in Gideon despite being sent to Zarahemla, why couldn't Pahoran send couriers who could've found Captain Moroni? The account written by Mormon fails to offer any kind of an explanation.

Following Pahoran's guidance, Captain Moroni left the northern armies under the leadership of Lehi and Teancum and took a small number of men to Gideon. Along the march, Captain Moroni carried out a recruiting drive, drawing thousands of men to strengthen the army at Gideon, though apparently this march took most of a year. The combined armies of Pahoran and Captain Moroni then assaulted Zarahemla at the end of the year (Alma 62:3–8), overwhelming the king men, who were led by a man named Pachus.

It's possible that they fought in the traditional way—meeting on a plain or appointed field outside the city—because the account says they approached the city and met the army of Pachus. It's possible that a siege was mounted, but the term *met* usually implies an encounter, in this case while they approached the city. Mormon doesn't describe the battle in detail, mentioning only that Pachus was killed, his army was defeated, and many prisoners were taken (Alma 62:7–8). Speedy trials were held for all those who wouldn't take an oath of support for the government, after which they were executed. Because of how the war started, no mercy was shown at all, and death sentences were speedily carried out. Obviously, there was a different definition of human rights in Nephite times. Mormon justified the speedy trials and large number of executions as necessary during a time of war (Alma 62:9–10). Today, Captain Moroni would probably be charged with war crimes and find himself put on trial for his actions. However, he was living under a different law then.

Once Pahoran was back in power in Zarahemla, Captain Moroni immediately dispatched six thousand men to reinforce Helaman and six thousand to Teancum and Lehi. The long-awaited reinforcements relieved the pressure on the beleaguered Nephite ranks on the front lines of both of these theaters (Alma 62:12–15). In the beginning of the thirty-first year of the reign of the judges (61 BC), Captain Moroni and Pahoran marched at the head of a new army to recover the city of Nephihah.

En route, they encountered a Lamanite army, perhaps being sent by Ammoron to link up with the king men in Zarahemla, though also possibly continuing the drive from Nephihah down the Sidon River valley. Regardless of its intended mission, the Lamanites seemed surprised to encounter such a strong Nephite army, which probably contributed to their quick defeat. This encounter may provide further support for the idea that Pachus's army unwisely fought an open engagement outside the walls of Zarahemla, rather than endure a siege, as the Lamanites probably expected to surprise a besieging Nephite army, not encounter one on an offensive march. Captain Moroni's army then confiscated the defeated Lamanite army's provisions and weapons. After making the prisoners take oaths of peace, he let them go. Again, the oath was a sufficient bond to prevent these men from taking up arms again (Alma 62:15–17).

Chapter 10: The Retaking of Nephihah

Captain Moroni's army continued its march until reaching the flat ground just outside Nephihah. After pitching their tents, they then followed convention by inviting the Lamanite garrison to come out to battle. The Lamanites, no doubt knowing and fearing Captain Moroni's reputation, refused.

Wanting to avoid a costly siege, Captain Moroni did some personal reconnaissance, climbing the city's defenses in order to see how the Lamanite forces were distributed within. He noted that the bulk of their men were positioned near the city entrance, which he recognized as a Lamanite weakness and an opportunity for his forces. Moroni went back to his camp, woke up his men, and had them hastily prepare ropes and ladders. Afterward, they approached a sector where there were no Lamanites and climbed into the city. In the morning, the Lamanites awoke to find Captain Moroni's army inside Nephihah, ready to fight. They fled toward the entrance, but Moroni's forces were covering this location as well. On Captain Moroni's order, his forces attacked, killing many of the Lamanites, capturing others, and scattering the rest into the wilderness of the land of Moroni. The account states that Captain Moroni didn't lose a single man on this mission (Alma 62:20–26).

It seems incredible that even with the bulk of Lamanite forces near the entrance that Lamanite sentries weren't placed along the fortifications around the city. Perhaps they were and Captain Moroni had the sentries along a specific section of the city eliminated, though this risked alerting the rest of the garrison and foiling Moroni's plan. On the other hand, it's more common than armies like to acknowledge that sentries fall asleep, especially in armies whose morale is low, or whose supply lines have been cut or weakened. Perhaps in Captain Moroni's reconnaissance, he found a sector where the guards were either sleeping or had failed to show up for duty. Finally, it's much easier than most people think for individuals and even small groups of men who are using stealth techniques to sneak into enemy positions at night, even heavily fortified positions, though the risk is quite high. Japanese ninjas and Vietnamese sappers are two groups who specialized in this skill.

It could also simply be an indication of just how bad things had gotten for the Lamanites. Attrition may have taken a serious toll on them, to the point that there weren't even enough forces to properly garrison the city's fortifications. The only actual military defeat of the Lamanites mentioned in the account at this time was the battle between Nephihah and Zarahemla, though there may have been a number of other engagements not reported because they were less important or less decisive. Another element often forgotten is how much non-combat causes, such as nutrition and disease, have impacted armies prior to the invention of modern medicine. For example, a major contributing factor to the conquest of Native American civilizations and tribes by the European explorers and settlers was their decimation by European diseases, from which the Native Americans had no immunity. The Lamanites in Nephihah may have been defeated by such a non-combat factor.

The most problematic issue in the account is one of timing. The time necessary to reconnoiter, prepare ropes and ladders, and infiltrate an army into a city all during one night seems improbable. It would be more plausible for it to have occurred over two nights with a day of preparation in between. Another problem with the account is the task of moving several thousand men into a city, all of them wearing battle gear, without being detected. The account implies that they crossed the wall of the fortifications at a point where the bulk of the Lamanites were absent, but even extremely disciplined and rehearsed

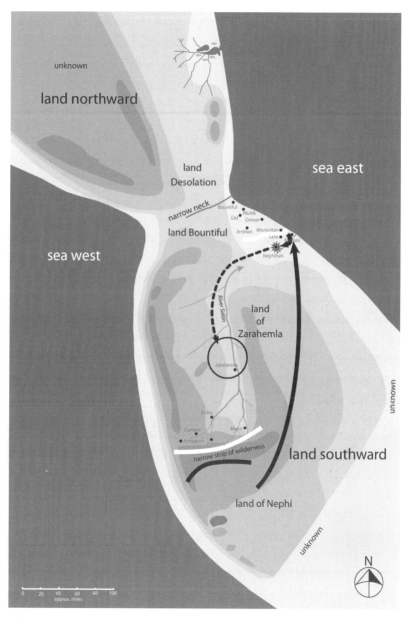

Third Lamanite Campaign: Battle of Nephihah. Based on *Mormon's Map*. Courtesy of John L. Sorenson (Provo: Farms, 2000).

men would be challenged to accomplish this feat without making at least some noticeable noise.

In this regard, the timing issue is problematic because, to avoid noise, Captain Moroni might have had his men muffle their equipment with cloth strips or some other means, techniques used repeatedly through history to mask noise. These preparations take time, again calling into question the timing described in the account. As it's described, it doesn't seem too plausible.

This is one of the few battle accounts in the Book of Mormon where the plausibility of the story is questionable as it is written. This doesn't indicate an error that falsifies the account and book. The details are missing here because Mormon didn't include them, which could indicate that maybe the source that Mormon abridged from contained the problematic information. Mormon probably transcribed it as he found it as he wasn't a witness to the event. Alternatively, it's possible that the original source was clear, but while in the process of abridging, Mormon garbled the account.

Despite the problematic details, in the larger picture, the important fact is that Nephihah was taken without loss to the Nephites, though the same can't be said for the Lamanites. This battle was a significant tipping point in the war, as it seemed to finally break the Lamanites' will to continue the fight.

An indication of their broken will in the text is the mention that many Lamanite prisoners wanted to join the people of Ammon.[14] They were allowed to do so, surely after taking an oath. Mormon states that this relieved the Nephites of all of their prisoners, a factor which may have aided the decision. The text again suffers from a lack of detail, as it's unclear as if this refers to all of the Lamanite prisoners, including the several thousand in Bountiful, or just to those captured at Nephihah.

Another question that arises is what happened to those prisoners who didn't decide to join the people of Ammon? Given the options available to military commanders at the time, a distinct possibility is that they were put to death. The account simply says that after this time there were no more Lamanite prisoners (Alma 62:27–29).

---

14. Ethnic Lamanites who had become incorporated into the Nephite polity.

Two-Pronged Drive to Moroni

The Battle of Nephihah so demoralized the Lamanites that when Moroni's army approached the land of Lehi, the Lamanites fled. This produced something of a chain reaction, with Lehi and Teancum driving from the north down the coast and Captain Moroni driving from the west in a southeast direction, with both forces vigorously pursuing the Lamanites and taking land after land and city after city until linking up just outside the land of Moroni.

The Lamanite armies had fled to this area, gathering in one body and being led by Ammoron, the Lamanite king himself, who hoped that his presence would shore up his men's morale.

The Nephite army formed an arc around the Lamanites in Moroni from the west and north. Because of the direction of their advances, Captain Moroni was probably on the west and Lehi and Teancum were likely on the north. Both armies were exhausted from hard marching and lack of sleep before the anticipated battle the next day. In fact, they were so exhausted that neither side developed any stratagem or ruse to beat the other, with the exception of Teancum (Alma 62:30–35).

The Battle of the Land of Moroni

Teancum decided to single-handedly end the war, perhaps feeling that a repeat of his earlier exploit—that is, assassinating Ammoron like he did Amalickiah—would end the war forthwith. He infiltrated the Lamanite camp, made his way to the king's tent, and thrust a javelin into his heart. However, unlike Amalickiah who died silently, Ammoron cried out in his death, which woke up his servants. These servants pursued Teancum and killed him (Alma 62:35–36).

Captain Moroni received the news of Teancum's death with great sadness, but Teancum's death provided a martyr figure for the Nephites. Conversely, Ammoron's death served to demoralize the Lamanites even further, removing any motivation to inspire them to fight. The scriptures state that when the battle started the next day, the Nephites attacked with fury and began slaying the Lamanite army "with great slaughter" (Alma 62:38), probably shouting something along the lines of, "Remember Teancum!"

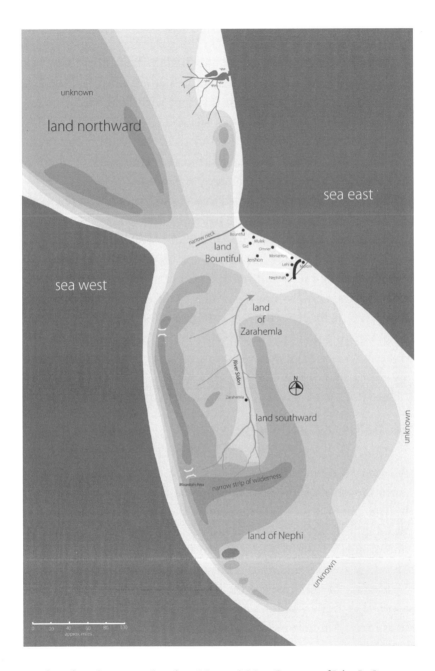

Final Nephite Campaign. Based on *Mormon's Map*. Courtesy of John L. Sorenson (Provo: Farms, 2000).

The Battle of the Land of Moroni marked the end of the war, as the Lamanite armies finally retreated, withdrawing completely from the lands of the Nephites. The great war was finally over.

Final Observations

Chapter 11: Post-War

In the thirty-second year, Moroni remained in command of the armies. His final task was to prepare the Nephite defenses for any possible future attack. This preparation probably included rebuilding cities that had changed hands during the war, rebuilding fortifications, and recruiting and training new soldiers. After restoring everything to his standards, he turned over command of his armies to his son Moronihah in that same year. Captain Moroni was only about thirty-nine years old at the time and Moronihah was probably somewhere between fourteen and twenty-four years old[15] when he assumed command. The Nephites apparently preferred their military commanders to be young.

Within four years, both (former) Captain Moroni and Helaman died (Alma 63:1–3). Captain Moroni was only forty-three years old at his death, probably indicating that his eighteen years of command had been physically hard on his body and that he may have died of complications from his war wounds. Helaman may have died from similar causes.

Like many modern post-war periods, the Nephite post-war period was a restless one. A man named Hagoth built several ships and people boarded them and migrated northward. People also began to migrate

---

15. Depending on how young his father was when he was born, Moronihah would've been twenty-five if his father had been fifteen—marriage often occurred young anciently—and fourteen if his father had been twenty-five.

north overland. This phenomenon enhances the authenticity of the account as it matches the post-war histories of many nations.

It's quite interesting that in US history, post-war periods have usually been periods of great upheaval and change, including large migrations in the aftermath of the Revolutionary War, the war with Mexico and the Civil War. World War I was followed by the Great Depression. The Vietnam War led to a cultural upheaval. Wars change societies and cause people to question the status quo. The Nephites were no different—twelve years of constant war had changed their society profoundly. This is a minor but significant detail that argues against Joseph Smith's authorship of the Book of Mormon.

Conclusion

The Book of Mormon accounts of the great war of Captain Moroni are fascinating, though they raise many questions. It's still something of a mystery why Mormon describes this war in so much detail when other wars are described scarcely or even not at all, their existence only inferred within the text.

If this is a spiritual book, one written by commandment, why was all of the strategic, operational, and tactical detail of this particular war necessary? The answer isn't clear and may be a combination of various factors. Assuming that the book was written to help people in these latter days, the great war of Captain Moroni has, for example, a clear parallel to the rise of Hitler and the titanic struggle of World War II. Certainly these chapters have helped members of the Church, no matter in what capacity they've served, to stay faithful through this trying conflict. It really wouldn't be surprising if the Lord commanded Mormon to include these chapters because He knew that World War II was coming, and perhaps other wars yet unseen but of equally titanic dimensions. However, still, while the general accounts were obviously important, why all the tactical detail? If the Book of Mormon was intended as a spiritual guide, that kind of detail doesn't seem particularly necessary.

Perhaps there's a much more mundane and non-spiritual reason, one that has little to do with the modern reader. The accounts may have been to provide Mormon himself with a guide for his military career. Its inclusion in the plates Mormon kept with him guaranteed that he would always have it to refer to as he sought guidance for his own military decisions. In addition, it would be a useful guide to Mormon's son, Moroni, also a military officer (see Mormon 6:12). By having the accounts on the plates, Moroni possessed a history of his namesake to refer to in his times of trouble.

However, would the Lord have made such a personal allowance? Certainly Mormon was forbidden to write other things that he wanted to—that appear to have been of a greater spiritual value—so why would God allow less spiritual things on the plates if not even intended for future readers? In the context of what we know about the golden plates, this explanation seems to fall short.

This leads to conclusion that there's another reason, perhaps one that we haven't been sophisticated enough to understand. Perhaps the great war of Captain Moroni was like the Peloponnesian War: a war like no other, a war that was transformational for Nephite society. It was in this war that the old patterns of ritualistic and heroic warfare were discarded and a new, more brutal and deadly form of warfare was adopted. This new form of war was one in which total domination and annihilation became the objective, thus setting the stage for the outcome for Nephite civilization—Christ's appearance and ministry in the New World only delaying this outcome for a couple hundred years. Such a pivotal war would merit description, but it's not clear (given the clarity of the remainder of the book) that God would be so cryptic about the importance of these accounts. More study needs to be undertaken on the purpose of the war accounts.

While the purpose of all this detail on warfare in a sacred text is still uncertain, what is certain is its existence provides solid support for the stance that Joseph Smith wasn't, nor were any of his contemporaries, the author of the Book of Mormon. The content of the book, as Joseph Smith claims, almost certainly came from another source. Whether one believes this other author was inspired of God or not is a separate matter, a matter of faith.

And what elements argue against Joseph Smith's authorship in the context of this study? First, whoever wrote these war accounts had a great deal of knowledge about military strategy, operations, tactics, and dynamics of war. They knew, for example, about the principle of escalation, the basic principle that war escalates as both sides act and react in the attempt to defeat the other. In the accounts, the Nephites issued armor to all of their troops, so the Lamanites adopted armor. The Nephites devised new forms of fortification and the Lamanites developed ways to overcome those fortifications and conquer numerous cities. To prevent the Nephites from retaking the cities, the Lamanites developed new defenses. The Nephites perfected maneuvering and deception, forcing the Lamanites to adopt countermeasures. And so on it goes. This is a subtle principle that someone who isn't versed in war—and even many who are—doesn't consciously use with ease. The fact that it's present in these war accounts is an indication of their authenticity.

Second, the accounts demonstrate the importance of terrain and its profound impact on military operations. Understanding terrain explains what offensive and defensive strategies each side chose and why. The Lamanite variations of simultaneous offensives up either coast were variations of what is known as the classic double envelopment, or "hammer-and-anvil approaches." Carrying out two-pronged assaults has inherent risks. It meant the Lamanites were moving along external lines, longer and more vulnerable, while the Nephite defenders were moving along internal lines: shorter, quicker, and more easily defended. The Nephites could and did shift forces from place to place as needed while the Lamanites could only move one direction at a time. For the Lamanites, it meant that communications between the two attacking armies wasn't good—if not impossible—at times, so coordination wasn't always possible. This favored the defending Nephites because they could shift forces and defeat the Lamanites while the other prong of the Lamanite army wouldn't know of the maneuvers or outcomes for days, neutralizing the double envelopment. All of these authentic dynamics and their effects appear in the text.

Third, the author of these accounts understood the importance of military logistics, one of the most remarkable elements that appear in the Book of Mormon. Logistics and logistical considerations figure prominently in these accounts. The various grand plans that the Lamanites adopted in their efforts to conquer the Nephite lands were sound and rational, from a logistical point of view. Why conduct a major campaign attacking up either coast? Because of the ease of supplying forces by boat (as explained earlier) versus hauling them on human backs. Attacks in the center of the land, such as the Battle of the City of Noah, were more reminiscent of raids that were meant to be quick, lightning strikes precisely because of the need to carry supplies on soldiers' backs or on the backs of porters, which made a prolonged campaign undesirable. In this manner, an offensive army could attack a given location, but couldn't maintain a siege or take possession of that site without establishing additional lines of logistics.

We see many additional references to logistics. Helaman begged for supplies; Captain Moroni threatened to overthrow the government if his forces didn't receive supplies; the Lamanites left their fortified city and pursued Helaman at Antiparah to prevent their logistics from being cut off; the Lamanites pursued Helaman again at Manti because he threatened their supply line; and the Lamanite line in the west collapsed because the main logistical hub of Manti was cut off. The accounts in the Book of Mormon and overall grasp of logistics underscores the fact that the author was no amateur. Napoleon has been widely reported to have invented the proverb: "Amateurs study tactics while professionals study logistics." The preoccupation in the Book of Mormon with logistics indicates that such a professional wrote the accounts.

These are just a few of the remarkable elements of war that appear in the text. Could someone who didn't have all of this knowledge (for even a section of the book) have made this story up? Highly unlikely. One of my professional jobs has been to design and run military exercises that involve creating realistic (though fictional) scenarios that take into account terrain, strategy, logistics, tactics, politics, and a whole host of other factors. These are seriously complex endeavors that require teams of people, writing, rewriting, negotiating, and editing for months. The team members are always a combination of the best and brightest military and civilian personnel with large amounts of operational experience, academic knowledge, and craft expertise—that is to say, they know the best ways to write scenarios.

Even so, it's still extremely difficult to write fictional scenarios that require the participant to suspend only a little reality when the games are played. The Holy Grail of military exercises is one with almost no suspension of reality and where the approximation to reality is nearly total. The greater the approximation to reality, the greater the benefits that the players get out of the exercise because they will take it more seriously. If this is a near impossible task for a team of the best and brightest military exercise designers to accomplish, then what does this say about Joseph Smith, or a combination of Joseph Smith, Oliver Cowdery, and perhaps others?

Some may think a more appropriate comparison is with someone like Tom Clancy, a writer of military fiction. Not true, because Tom Clancy doesn't pretend that his stories are reality, and since the reader understands this, he or she can simply enjoy the ride. There are many obviously fantastic and outrageous elements in Tom Clancy's novels, but he isn't punished for these elements because everyone understands that the story is fictional.

But the Book of Mormon, on the other hand, claims to be real. While fictional exercise scenarios don't pretend to be real either, they attempt to be as real as possible so that the players will treat them as if they were real and act accordingly. The value of the exercise is the training that's obtained in order to prepare the participant to act in a real situation. It's the complexity of writing all of the overt and subtle dynamics into a fictional scenario that make this such a difficult task. The Book of Mormon combines all of these elements seamlessly. It's extremely difficult to believe, in this context, that this could be fiction concocted by someone like Joseph Smith or any of his contemporaries from the nineteenth century, writing about a war that was supposed to have taken place in the first century BC.

As stated before, there are minor and occasional—not major and consistent—problems with Mormon's account of Captain Moroni's war. For example, there are problems with the accounts of the battles that took place for the cities of Gid and the Nephihah, both analyzed earlier, as specific details appear not to coincide with reality. Some of the claims that Mormon makes seem a bit fantastic, though the accounts are plausible if modified slightly, as previously noted. In other words, the problems may be problems of clarity rather than problems of substance. Mormon didn't give us more information, so we can't know for sure.

However, both of these problematic accounts occur at the end of the narrative of the great war. Perhaps the abridger, Mormon, was a bit tired and not completely careful when writing the stories of these battles. He may have been near the end and in a hurry, so he didn't entirely think through the writing or provide careful details, like those contained in the earlier battle accounts. In other words, this may be a case of writer fatigue, a factor that may actually enhance rather than detract from the authenticity of the account because it shows that a real person who was subject to real stresses wrote the account.

There are probably many other things that could be pointed to as evidence for the authenticity of the accounts and against Joseph Smith's authorship. I have named only some of the more important ones. They certainly have convinced me that Joseph Smith wasn't the author and helped confirm my belief that the Book of Mormon is what it claims to be and what Joseph Smith said it is: the translation of an ancient text revealed to him by God. Certainly the complex military dynamics in the book further enhance this argument.

Ultimately, however, it's incumbent on each person to discover for themselves whether the work is of God or not. I have sought to add one more plank to the argument that Joseph Smith wasn't the author of the Book of Mormon, and thus further enhance the plausibility that it's an authentic sacred text.

Bonus Content

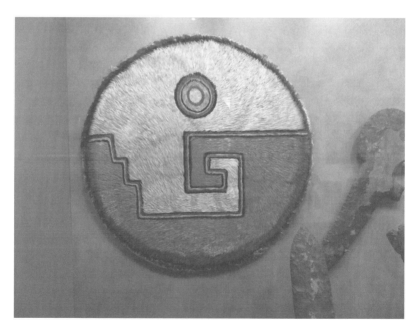

An Aztec shield with elaborate feather design, which means that it was probably ceremonial. (Mexico City, Museum of Anthropology. Photo: David Spencer.)

A battle scene carved in the base of a large platform stone in which an Aztec warrior (left) takes a captive (right), symbolized by the Aztec warrior's grip on the other warrior's hair. Both warriors are armed with spear throwers. The Aztec warrior wears an elaborate helmet, a heavy collar to protect his neck from blows, a bird effigy breastplate, and a shield. The other has a less elaborate headdress, a protective collar, no breastplate, and no shield. Both warrior's legs are essentially unprotected. (Mexico City, Museum of Anthropology. Photo: David Spencer.)

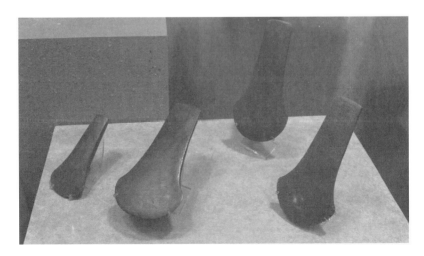

Bronze axe heads that were used in battle. Bronze and stone blades were used simultaneously. (Mexico City, Museum of Anthropology. Photo: David Spencer.)

Aztec warrior pillar, front and back. His headdress is a large eagle effigy head plate. A somewhat larger plate covers his breast. In addition, his forearms are covered with bracelets that go all the way up to his elbows, perhaps meant as some kind of protection. His legs below his knees are similarly covered. He holds spears for his *atlatl*, or spear thrower, which is unseen in his other hand. His shield is on his back. The skirt hanging down from the shield may be more than just decoration, possibly serving as protection against blows or projectiles to the legs. (Mexico City, Museum of Anthropology. Photo: David Spencer.)

An Aztec sketch showing a bronze axe being used in battle. The figure is armored with either a heavy protective collar or a breastplate and a round shield. (Mexico City, Museum of Anthropology. Photo: David Spencer.)

Photo of the bastioned walls of Cahokia in Illinois. Though Mississippian mound cities had fortifications remarkably similar to the descriptions of fortifications in the Book of Mormon, I haven't felt these were Book of Mormon locations. The dates don't match and the Book of Mormon never mentions winters with snow (a major feature in all historic accounts from northern climate cultures). However, given the similarities, it's possible that Mississippian culture was inspired by Book of Mormon peoples. (Cahokia Mounds Stake Historic Site. Photo: David Spencer.)

A drawing of the bastioned walls of Cahokia mound site in Illinois. (Cahokia Mounds Stake Historic Site. Photo: David Spencer.)

A drawing of a warrior with chest armor and a "helmet" made of woven material of some kind. (Cahokia Mounds Stake Historic Site. Photo: David Spencer.)

A depiction of the walled main temple compound at Cahokia, Illinois. (Cahokia Mounds Stake Historic Site. Photo: David Spencer.)

A Mayan warlord stands over a captured enemy. He has an armored shield that goes around his neck to cover his front. It is secured at his waist. His weapon appears to be a serrated lance. (Mexico City, Museum of Anthropology. Photo: David Spencer.)

Bench supports from the warrior's city of Tula. The one on the left wears a kind of scale armor and a helmet. The one on the right wears a thick collar over a breast shield that covers his torso and crotch. (Mexico City, Museum of Anthropology. Photo: David Spencer.)

These ceramic figure tomb offerings came from a culture on the west coast of Mexico, in the states of Jalisco, Nayarit, Colima, Michoacán, and Zacatecas. The culture likely existed between 300 BC and AD 600. The figures are distinguished by their cylindrical body armor and their combed helmets, making them almost look Greek. (Mexico City, Museum of Anthropology. Photo: David Spencer.)

More ceramic figurines from the same culture. The warrior with the full-length shield seems to be wielding a lance, but that part is broken. The figure with a small round shield slung on his back is wielding a projectile weapon, either a sling or a broken bow. (Mexico City, Museum of Anthropology. Photo: David Spencer.)

A warrior figurine from the same culture. He has a thick quilted armored shirt, arm and shin guards, a shield, a lance, and a really elaborate reptile helmet. (Mexico City, Museum of Anthropology. Photo: David Spencer.)

Another painted figurine. Next to him are two stone mace heads, seemingly a favorite weapon of this culture. (Mexico City, Museum of Anthropology. Photo: David Spencer.)

About the Author

D r. David Spencer is a professor of counterterrorism and counterinsurgency at the William J. Perry Center for Hemispheric Defense Studies, where he teaches courses on defense and security to government and private individuals from US partner nations. While at the center, Dr. Spencer has been assigned to serve details at the Office of the Secretary of Defense, first in the Office of Western Hemisphere Affairs and more recently in the Office of Counternarcotics and Global Threats. For his performance at OSD, he was awarded the Exceptional Public Service Medal in 2013.

Dr. Spencer earned his doctorate in political science from George Washington University in 2002, where he studied Latin American politics, specializing in regional insurgency and terrorism. He earned his master's and bachelor's in international relations from Brigham Young University in 1992 and 1988, respectively.

David was director of combating terrorism at Hicks & Associates. Most of his work over the last twenty years has been supporting different aspects of US government policy in Colombia. Before that, he spent five years in El Salvador as a consultant to the Ministry of Defense during the 1979–92 civil war.

David was raised in Latin America, living in Chile, Costa Rica, Colombia, Venezuela, and Guatemala. He served in the US Army and National Guard as a combat engineer and as an infantryman. He attained the rank of sergeant and was mobilized for the first Gulf War in 1990–91.

His other publications include *Colombia's Road to Recovery: Security and Governance 1982–2010*, *Guerra El Salvador-Honduras Ilustrada*, *Improvizirana Oklopna Vozila 1991–95*, *Hrvatski Orlovi: Paratroopers of the Independent State of Croatia 1942–45*, *From Vietnam to El Salvador: The Saga of the FMLN Sappers and other Guerrilla Special Forces in Latin America*, *Strategy and Tactics of the Salvadoran FMLN Guerrillas: Last Battle of the Cold War, Blueprint for Future Conflicts*, and *Armored Fighting Vehicles of El Salvador*.